Finding True Inner Comfort

Being Praised

Finding True Inner Comfort is a thought-provoking spiritual journey to "being" our authentic selves. Dr. Don's exploration of the seven principles of *The Kybalion* will compel you to recognize that "we are love, peace, and joy at the very core." Practicing these principles undoubtedly will produce lifelong contentment.
—MARILYN RULE

One of those books that only comes around once in a great while, *Finding True Inner Comfort* explains the big questions of life. It encourages one to look deeper into oneself as it expands our knowledge of our Creator; a Creator that even an atheist could love. It carefully presents profound ideas for healing. While not a religious book, it certainly touched my soul and enlightened my heart.
—REV. JOSE A. HERNAIZ

This is a book that I kept picking up after slowly chewing on the delicious morsels of wisdom. As I kept reading *Finding True Inner Comfort*, I got into the flow of its messages, as they deeply resonated within me. The principles explained in it have added significantly to my spiritual growth and expanded my understanding of how life works.
—CONNIE NUHFER

Finding True Inner Comfort is a calm, yet powerful, life-changing voice of hope and reason within the growing crisis of addiction.
—L. S. KERR, MS

Finding True Inner Comfort

Dr. Don W. Jones

FINDING TRUE INNER COMFORT
More being, less doing

WITH ANCIENT AND TIMELESS WISDOM FROM THE KYBALION

Copyrighted Material

Finding True Inner Comfort: More being, less doing

Copyright © 2019 by Don W. Jones.
All Rights Reserved.

All rights are reserved. No part of this book is to be reproduced by any digital, mechanical, photographic, or electronic process, or in the form of any phonographic recording, digital or otherwise; nor may it be stored in a retrieval system, transmitted, or otherwise be copied or duplicated for public or private use—other than for "fair use" as brief quotations expressed in articles and reviews within any medium without prior written permission of the author.

The author of this book does not give medical advice or prescribe the use of any technique as a type of treatment for physical or medical problems, including mental health without the advice of a licensed medical professional, either directly or indirectly. The intent of the author is limited to offering general information of the purpose of helping in your pursuit of improved daily living and spiritual well-being. On any occasion that you might use any of the information in this book for your own life improvement, which is your constitutional right, the author and the publisher assume no responsibility.

For information about this title or to order other books
and/or electronic media, contact the publisher:

GraySpace Press
PO Box 140333
Toledo, Ohio 43614
drdonwjones.com
grayspacepress@gmail.com

Library of Congress Cataloging-in-Publication Data

Reference: Personal Growth / Spiritual / Addiction
031000 032000 026000

ISBNs
Softcover: 978-1-7335962-0-6
eBook: 978-1-7335962-1-3

Published and distributed in the United States by GraySpace Press

Editorial Assistance by: Don Lee

Cover and Illustration Designs: Mark Ruffner

Being Dedicated

This book is dedicated to the Three Initiates, who chose to anonymously publish the book known as *The Kybalion* in order to solidify the seven ancient principles for the modern world.

It is also dedicated to all those who heroically pursue enlightenment and an awakening that truly satisfies and heals life's discomforts.

Being Acknowledged

Special acknowledgments go to Kathy, whose life and death helped propel my own lifetime pursuit for the solutions to mental and emotional pain; to my sister, who has endlessly supported me through all aspects of my life; to John, whose words of encouragement ignited the fire in me to write this book; and to all my teachers, including family, friends, patients, and clients. This book would not exist without our manifested spiritual connections.

The actual production of this book could not have taken place without the technical and design skills of many others. Special acknowledgment goes to Don Lee who knows how the English language and grammar should be presented. And I give a huge thank you to Mark Ruffner for the amazing designs contained within the pages of *Finding True Inner Comfort* and for the inspiring cover designs—talent and skill united!

And the biggest shout-out is to Tony, who is the most authentic person I have had the honor and pleasure to know—*really* know.

Contents

Foreword by J. R. Maxon   xvii
Introduction by Dr. Don W. Jones   xix

Chapter One: Being Searchers   **1**
   Finding the Elusive Key to Living   2
   A Changed Way of Living   4
   Interpreting the Seven Principles   5
   Our Sources   6
   Life Source Illustration   7
   "Out There" Sources   8
   Inner Self Source   9
   The Bridging Tools   10
   Imposter Comfort   11
      Lilly's Story   11
      Review Points   12
      Affirmations of Intention   13

Chapter Two: Being Busy — 15
    Survival Comfort-seeking — 16
    Distraction Comfort-seeking — 16
    Automatic Comfort-seeking — 17
        Dean's Story — 18
    Automatic Comforting That Is Addiction — 19
        Bryan's Story — 20
        Thoughts and Beliefs — 21
    True Inner Comfort — 21
        Review Points — 23
        Affirmative Prayer of Intention — 24

Chapter Three: Being Mind — 25
    Donovan's Story — 28
    What Can Be Changed Is Our Thinking — 30
    All Is Becoming, Nothing Is — 31
        Review Points — 32
        Affirmative Prayer for Acceptance — 33

Chapter Four: Being In The All — 35
    The Physical Plane — 37
    The Mental Plane — 37
    The Spiritual Plane — 38
    Satisfaction Related to Correspondence — 39
    Original Sin—Fact or Fiction? — 41
    The Question of Heaven and Hell — 42
    A Look at Below — 43
        Odela's Story — 46
        Review Points — 47
        Affirmations for Higher Intentions — 48

Chapter Five: Highest Being — **51**

Raising Vibrations — 52
Focusing on the Negative — 54
Blocked Vibration: Question Perceptions — 55
   Letting Go — 56
   Letting God — 58
Tools for Change — 59
Innate Tools for Change — 60
Mental Tools for Change — 60
   Thoughts — 60
   Prayer — 61
   Visualization — 61
   Affirmations — 62
   Masterminding — 62
   Positive Thinking — 63
   Mindfulness and Meditation — 64
Emotive Tools for Change — 65
   Gratitude — 65
   Forgiveness — 67
   Compassion — 68
   Love — 68
Being Tools for Change — 69
   Being Love — 70
   Being Kindness — 70
   Being Open-minded — 71
   Being Authentic — 71
   Neal's Story — 72
   Review Points — 73
   Affirmations — 74
   Mindful Meditation Examples — 75

Chapter Six: Being This and That — 79

A Quick Breakdown of This and That — 80
Duality Versus Polarity — 81
Yin Yang Redesign Illustration — 82
Paradoxes Reconciled — 84
A Short Trip to Eden — 85
Freedom of Choice in Direction — 88
Consciously Living within the Continuum — 90
- *Jackson's Story* — 91
- *Is That So?* — 92
- *The Moral of the Story* — 93

Visualize Getting Jacked Up — 94
Final Thoughts on Polarity — 95
- *Review Points* — 96
- *Guided Meditation* — 97

Chapter Seven: Being Confident — 101

Three Planes of Rhythm — 102
- *Physical-plane Rhythm* — 102
- *Mental-plane Rhythm* — 102
- *Spiritual-plane Rhythm* — 103

Perceived Lack of Control — 104
Conscious Addressing of Negative Thoughts — 105
Neutralization — 107
Transmutation of Unsound Beliefs — 108
Cognitive Behavioral Therapy — 109
Refusing to Participate — 112
Law of Compensation — 115
Negative to Positive Inclination — 116
- *Review Points* — 116
- *Belief Transformation Exercise* — 117
- *Do-It-Yourself CBT Worksheet* — 118

Chapter Eight: Being Creative — 121
- A Fallen Tree Limb — 122
- Karma — 123
  - *Childlessness Caused Cancer?* — 124
- Luck and Chance — 125
  - *Gambling and Chance* — 126
- Blessings and Grace — 127
- Fate, Predestination, and Predetermination — 129
  - *The Lesson of the Bicyclists* — 130
  - *Fate with Flexibility* — 131
  - *"I guess it was not meant to be."* — 133
  - *Supposed To* — 133
  - *What God Wants?* — 134
- Listening and Looking for Signs — 135
- Masters of Our Fate — 136
  - *Review Points* — 137
  - *Affirmative Prayer* — 137

Chapter Nine: Being Authentic — 139
- Gender Is Not the Same as Sex — 140
- The Nature of The All — 140
- The Root of Most Human Suffering — 141
- Principle of Gender Distinctions (table) — 143
- We Are Taught Lies — 144
- What Is the Truth — 145
- Lack of Authenticity Is Crippling — 146
- It Starts with Gender Imbalances — 148
- Battle of the Sexes — 149
- Achieving Gender Balance — 152
  - *Review Points* — 154
  - *Affirmative Prayer* — 155

Chapter Ten: Being Whole   **159**

    Seven Principles Summary   160
    Principle of Mentalism   161
    Principle of Correspondence   162
    Principle of Vibration   163
    Principle of Polarity   164
    Principle of Rhythm   165
    Principle of Cause and Effect   166
    Principle of Gender   167
    More Than Just Comfort-seeking Tools   168
    The Bigger Question in Life   169
        Our "Out There" Purpose in Life   169
        An Inner Purpose in Life   170
        Sam's Story   172
    The Seven Principles' Ultimate Gift   173
        Prayer to Self and The All   176
        A Guided Meditation   177

Author Biography—Being the Author   181

Foreword

The book you are holding presents a system of the most powerful and enlightening tools known to modern man. Based on ancient philosophies, with a contemporary explanation, *Finding True Inner Comfort* contains priceless information that will transform anyone's life. If I had to select one book to take on my spiritual journey, it would be this one. It is a book for awakening the reader and also provides a convenient everyday reference. In it, Dr. Don not only shares the transforming lessons of his own life journey, but also he vividly presents compelling stories of others who have found themselves dissatisfied and struggling.

Packaging the wisdom and lessons he learned from the timeless principles of *The Kybalion*, he focuses on using these valuable tools for the purpose of helping those who find themselves at a painfully stuck point in their lives. In doing so, Dr. Don has created a beneficial and wonderful guide for learning how to find true *inner* comfort, instead of wasting time and energy searching for satisfaction in the usual, and always ineffective, *outer* world comforters.

FINDING TRUE INNER COMFORT

Everything needed for developing and enjoying a happy life is in *The Kybalion*. It is profound, ancient, and written in a colorful poetic script. With skill and clarity, Dr. Don simplifies and expands those comforting words of wisdom with an emphasis on guiding the reader in the discovery of their own inner power of love, peace, and joy.

I had the pleasure of attending Dr. Don's series of talks that led him to *Finding True Inner Comfort* and was one of the many students who encouraged him to put his teachings together in this book. As compelling and rewarding as his lectures were, I find myself being in awe of the book's many components that could not be conveyed in other than written form. From the many true-life stories, the clarifying Life Source illustration, the Do-It-Yourself worksheet, and the numerous other easy-to-use tools, I grew both mentally and spiritually from both reading and applying the truths found in *Finding True Inner Comfort*. This book is truly inspiring!

The knowledge contained in this book makes it a must-read for anyone seeking to grow and develop an illuminated spirituality, to advance their life of sobriety, and/or find a new pain-free way to live.

I am genuinely honored to encourage you to allow the truths and tools of *Finding True Inner Comfort* to find their way into your own story of success. It is success *worthy* of your effort.

—J. R. Maxon
   Author of *ReBecoming: The Way of Opportunity*

Introduction

Spring flowers are not yet displaying themselves as I sit here looking out of my dining room windows. The new sprouts are visible in the promise of the annual springtime blooming event. As I visualize this post-winter display, I contemplate the presentation of this book to an audience that is anxious for lasting comfort from the painful dis-ease of daily living; and it seems natural to appreciate the seasonal Laws of Nature as being somewhat simliar. Being predictable after a long winter, nature's show brings its own anxious anticipation for spring's stunning delivery. In a similar way, this book is finding its delivery after a long, creative, and productive process.

Finding True Inner Comfort is an exploration of the predictable physical Laws of Nature. It is also the unexpected and stunning mental and spiritual laws as found in the little-known, ancient principles originated in *The Kybalion*. How exciting it is to consider the holistic rewards the readers of this book can experience. They can find solutions that are newly embraced by science, and grounded in the poetic words that began being passed on hermetically eons ago! My own discovery of *The Kybalion* was nothing short of mind-boggling, so passing it on is thrilling for me.

My own search for answers for finding lasting relief in life began as a troubled teenager who just wanted the pain of rejection and dismissal to go away. Studying behavioral theory, psychology, and spiritual truisms as an adult has resulted in finding a lot of answers that I feel compelled to share. As a key part of that, I have long felt that the wisdom of the seven principles deserves a larger audience.

Even before I discovered *The Kybalion* I started the discussion in two other manuscripts. I had completed one manuscript and almost finished a second one when a series of unexpected events happened. Just as I was pulling my thoughts together for the final and most compelling chapter of that second manuscript, I found myself deeply dissatisfied with the previous chapters. The final chapter was to focus on the "being" aspects of a spiritually based cognitive therapy. At the time, the prospects of the final chapter vastly overshadowed the first chapters. This overshadowing was to such a degree that I lost interest in the manuscript as a whole. The abandoned keyboard was not the typical writer's block.

Within a week of my sudden lack of enthusiasm for that document, my house was burglarized. The only things taken: a broken cellphone and my laptop along with the attached flash drive. Among other writings, this laptop contained the electronic versions of my master's thesis, my doctoral dissertation, and, seemingly prophetic, the only versions of both self-help manuscripts. Backing up computer documents "in the cloud" was not in my awareness then, and I had only backed up my documents in the stolen flash drive.

While there was a sense of loss of all this intellectual property, I did see a sign of what new possibilities could spring from the event.

INTRODUCTION

The "being" aspect I was about to compile in the last chapter of the incomplete manuscript ended up planting the seed for writing an all-new manuscript—one that was fully devoted to "being."

As a bonus, the loss of those "identity" intellectual achievements really created an opportunity for me to fully realize that my true identity was not found in my degrees, papers, and manuscripts; I was reminded that my own true identity is found within myself. This is a critical aspect of *Finding True Inner Comfort*.

Continuing the foretelling nature of this shift, it was within a few days of the burglary that I discovered the little-known and powerful book called *The Kybalion*. This collection of seven ancient spiritually based principles clearly correlated with my "being" topic. The principles so impressed me that I began a series of nine Sunday talks at the Center for Conscious Living of Northwest Ohio, where I was spiritual director. As an addiction clinician, I focused my talks on how to find real and satisfying comfort in life as related to the knowledge found in those seven principles. Over and over, I heard members of the audience tell me that my spin on those principles should be turned into a book. Although I did not immediately begin the manuscript, I did get inspired to turn the notes from the talks into the manuscript for *Finding True Inner Comfort*. It has been a blissful and rewarding effort. The process did indeed clarify, deepen, and even expand the "being" understandings that I already had.

There is a deep satisfaction in compiling the many lessons of my life, the enlightening study of *The Kybalion*, and especially the hundreds of lessons from the lives of my patients, who are also my teachers. One such teacher helped me see just how devastating it can be for people to look for satisfaction and excitement in the wrong places. He was an inmate in a prison where I worked as an addiction counselor. This man was particularly pleasant and insightful at the time that I met him. One day I asked him if he had ever thought about how he got started in his life of crime and drugs. A knowing twinkle came to his eyes. He stated, "It started with throwing snowballs at cars when I was a kid. I got such a rush when the drivers got upset. But the snow melted and I wanted the thrills to continue. I started throwing stones. The reactions were even more thrilling. I just kept finding more thrilling things as I got older and ended up breaking the law. To be honest, I am more addicted to thrill-seeking than I am to drugs. And here I am with almost fifteen years of my life in and out of prison." This man's snowball throwing really did snowball in the worst possible ways.

Creating a body of work that presents key points for finding freedom from painful and stuck ways of living is greatly rewarding on many levels. I feel excitement in crafting a how-to guide for everyone who longs to lead a life that is liberated, comforted, and healthy. Learning the Laws of Nature, of our Source, as outlined in the ancient principles of *The Kybalion,* enriched my own awakening. It has, indeed, proved itself a journey worth taking.

It is my sincere hope that the readers of *Finding True Inner Comfort* discover their own "being" path in life; a life that is about the energies of more being and less doing. Introducing these ideas to my patients over the years has helped them to live life on its own terms, to enrich their spirits, and to free their minds. I have watched people living in this "being" place manifest profoundly satisfying transformations. No longer suffering the effects from harmful habits, mental dis-ease, and addiction, these brave souls have found an inner satisfaction that has always been at hand; they have uncovered their true selves as they reveal both inner and outer authenticity.

INTRODUCTION

For me, the manifestation of *Finding True Inner Comfort* feels like the fruition of a lifelong process from at least four sources: from life's lessons; from formal education; from a personal spiritual quest in life; and from the serendipitous discoveries found in knowledge gained from countless books, including *The Kybalion*. I am confident that implementation of the ideas presented here will allow anyone the wondrous opportunity to experience the inner love, peace, and joy that are found naturally inside his or her very own being.

Even though the seven principles found the ears of religious icons over the generations, we are talking about a set of principles that were never meant to be worshipped. The ideas were meant for understanding and utilizing. It is a tribute to their validity that they remain so to this day even though much of the book's teachings are found in all the world's religions. Even more legitimizing, those ideas are now found in modern scientific journals, as well.

While some people see the seven principles to be a study of the science of spirituality, others contend it seems more like exposing the spirituality of science. Either way, or both, I find that the understanding of those principles is a collection of tools for life. Many believe that its merits embrace most of the world's religions, acting as a collection of uniting umbrella philosophies. Indeed, I can see those principles complementing the teachings of our world's religious founders. I present them here with that in mind.

As we begin this narrow study of *The Kybalion*, consider the following quote from its first chapter:

> "So that according to the teachings, the passage of this book to those ready for the instruction will attract the attention of such as are prepared to receive the teaching. And

> likewise, when the pupil is ready to receive the truth, then will this little book come to him or her. Such is the Law. The Hermetic Principle of Cause and Effect, in its aspect of the Law of Attraction, will bring lips and ear together—pupil and book in company. So mote it be!"

The authors of *The Kybalion* were careful in making a clear distinction between the sacred handed-down principles versus the authors' interpretations and explanations. I have made every effort in *Finding True Inner Comfort* to do the same. You will note that I use quotation marks and a different font for the quotes taken from the publication. Those quotes that directly reference the words of the seven principles themselves are noted with the same font in bold type and reference—*The Kybalion*.

Out of tradition and respect, in referencing the Source of all things, I capitalize the first letter of each of those references, even those that are not traditional terms and names. That includes Creator, Higher Power, and Laws of Nature. "The All," which is the term used for an expanded understanding of God in *The Kybalion*, falls into that category. Just as the authors of that book do, I capitalize both words of that reference. When you see a word with the first letter capitalized, it most likely is one of the many terms referring to the Divine Creator.

At the end of each chapter of *Finding True Inner Comfort*, I present a set of Review Points and Bridging Tool exercises. It is my hope that these and other structures incorporated within allow this guide to be a quick reference piece as well as a thought-provoking read. No-border-line text boxes, generous descriptive subtitles, and real-life examples can be used for reference purposes.

INTRODUCTION

This specialized study of *The Kybalion* does not attempt to be a comprehensive study of its principles, but instead pulls carefully chosen key points that can help build a life that is joyful, love-filled, and in harmony—a comforted life. With this knowledge you can be all that!

CHAPTER ONE

Being Searchers

No one would disagree that life is a daily barrage of stressors, disappointments, and shocking events. These outer forces often compel us to find comfort in any manner we can. With the possible exception of a few spiritual gurus, people seek in the logical and traditional places; they look for satisfaction in the material world. Even though there are amazing inner qualities that bring us contentment and even joy, we look "out there" instead. These outer solutions are temporary. Most of us do not know how to find that inner comfort that is lasting.

Along the way of life, we may hear that people have some sort of inner beauty. Ancient philosophies not only accept that we have inner perfection; they inform us that we have inner power—the same powers as our Creator. These powers make us feel good—if we tap into them.

Even as a teenager I sought out some form of hidden knowledge that could help me feel less miserable. In middle school I read my dad's *Book of Knowledge* collection—every word of every book of the set. In high school I scoured the *World Book Encyclopedia*. By the time I entered undergraduate school I was devouring every philosophic and inspirational book, online source, and lecturer I could find. I learned a lot. But the elusive answer to finding ongoing joy, or even just contentment, long remained unfound.

As an adult I became interested in the old sages, such as Socrates, Plato, and the others. I studied the teachings of Jesus, Buddha, and more contemporary authorities, speakers, and authors. From them I gathered a surface-level mastery of life. It was as if I had all the knowledge I needed, but somehow all the elements swirled around, remained unsettled, and, therefore, were strangely elusive for practical use. I learned that I was not alone in this. I preached about seeking the truth, spoke of those Truths, and still felt I had not nailed it down. The search continued even as I used my many tools and passed those tools on to my patients and other hungry souls.

There was a part of me that just knew that I would find something that would help lock it all in real lasting results. My craving for comfort kept me ever-watchful for clues, answers, and even a magic bullet. Little did I know that the answer was in a little-known book based on five-thousand-year-old philosophies. This was not only important to me for my own satisfaction in life, it was essential for passing on to my patients and clients in my professional life.

Finding the Elusive Key to Living

It was at a rather critical time of my life, that I ran into the ancient set of philosophic principles that immediately rang true. The seven axioms seemed to be the original building blocks for most, if not all, the world's organized religions; and are a basic foundation for the science of life. These ideas were older than Moses, yet fresh in their simplicity. Uncomplicated by belabored expansion and many hidden-agenda dogmas, the statements of the principles are, indeed, eye-opening. It was an undiluted teaching. For me the ideas were familiar, but somehow were presented in such a way that, with a little thought, its wisdom nailed down the learned notions I had gathered over my lifetime.

It is fascinating that these very early principles had been passed on by word of mouth and known by just a few masters in any given generation. The origins of *The Kybalion* principles are said to be from Hermes. His ideas are said to have crossed continents even during his lifetime. Hermes was known by the Egyptians as the scribe of the gods, by Greeks as the god of wisdom, and ancient Romans as Mercury. Perhaps the power of the seven principles ultimately has Hermes to be known as the master of masters.

After centuries of secret verbal passage, these ideas were first published anonymously just over a century ago in the 1908 book called *The Kybalion*. The name's meaning is long lost, but its message is important as the philosophy explains how to be in vibrational synchronicity with our universe—which is key to taking control of our lives and finding comfort. This comfort leads to lives that are satisfying even in the midst of chaos.

Implementation of the knowledge found in the principles is a master's way to happiness. Somehow neither the book known as *The Kybalion,* nor the seven principles known by the same name, made it to global fame. This wisdom, which is subtitled *A Study of the Hermetic Philosophy of Ancient Egypt and Greece,* never became a religion in and of itself. It seems that it supersedes religion as its seven principles are part of the original teachings of most spiritual traditions and many of today's independent spiritual philosophies.

It is fortunate that the knowledge found in the seven principles allows all of us to be masters of happiness. With one principle building on the other, these seven Laws of Nature contain the information we need for finding true inner comfort from all our daily discomforts. While the ancient principles are a collection of ideas that explain the nature of the universe, they are also an attempt to explain our creation, our creative nature, and our Creator. Even those of us not so sure about the true existence of a Higher Power are given the opportunity to see life in a new and perhaps reassuring way.

A Changed Way of Living

The knowledge I gained, along with my studied conclusions from this discovery, helped my ability to remember to look inward more often; to have most of my daily efforts come from *being* rather than *doing*. Understanding the principles found in this book, and how they work in life, was astounding to me. It more than doubled my success in avoiding the frustrated *doing* place and staying in the *being* place. The age-old philosophic principles found in *The Kybalion* solidified the desired inward journey. This created a keen desire to share with others my new-found tools.

As a behavioral health professional with a dedicated spiritual path, I realized I had stumbled upon seven keys to helping break the cycle of addiction relapses for my clients. This led to the realization that knowledge of and use of these same seven principles had the potential to shift the level of consciousness of anyone stuck in any struggle of life. The conclusions I made from the study of *The Kybalion* became a great source toward ending pursuits of comfort *seeking* and leading to inner comfort *finding*.

The many "truths" that I discovered in *The Kybalion* helped me shift my consciousness. I transformed my consciousness by way of a different understanding of the nature of God, Allah, Mother Nature, Higher Self, the Force, or whatever term one refers to for the Higher Power of life. I learned that all things are energy-based. Even my nonreligious clients and those who professed to be atheists embraced these powerful ideas.

The authors wanted to remain anonymous. They referred to themselves as the Three Initiates, with the understanding that those who are ready for the knowledge will be led to their words. They stated:

"The lips of wisdom are closed, except to the ears of understanding."

Interpreting the Seven Principles

In *Finding True Inner Comfort*, I focus on the conclusions I have drawn from *The Kybalion* principles that help us establish a foundation of life of authentic contentment. They promote an avenue that is healthy and powerful and fulfilling.

The Kybalion is broken down into a study of seven principles. I use the same seven axioms of that book in revealing those aspects that are related to *Finding True Inner Comfort*. As exciting as the principles are, I don't want us to get ahead of ourselves. Before we get into those amazing tenets we must have a basic framework about the structure of how life works.

While that framework is not explicitly detailed in *The Kybalion*, the overall conclusions of the book embrace it. The rest of this chapter will help you gain an understanding of ideas that act as the foundation for using the seven principles of *The Kybalion*.

Toward that end, on the next page, I introduce a key description by way of an illustration called our Life Source. Based on ideas gathered over years of spiritual study, and supported by the overall deductions of *The Kybalion*, it outlines how life works. It gives a visual of the ideas that heretofore have been elusive to most of us. It helps us see the very basic nature of how we typically operate in life, as it illustrates how we can create a more effective way of living.

Our Sources

Life is mostly about seeking and finding comfort. We make many types of adjustments in order to find hundreds of kinds of gratification. With all this comfort-seeking, it would seem that at some point we would find satisfaction long enough to take a rest. For most of us, however, this type of seeking seems to be never-ending. For some of us, the search for relief has become problematic.

The premise of *Finding True Inner Comfort* is simple: lasting and meaningful satisfaction from the large and small everyday upsets of life are found *within* our own being. Contrary to what we are generally taught, it is not found in the endless number of temporary comforters found *outside* ourselves. Of course, there is nothing wrong with this fleeting source of solace. The problem is that the land of milk and honey is not found *outside* ourselves in the short-term remedies; those that have the tendency to need repeating. This over and over again process is such that we seek an

BEING SEARCHERS

Life Source

endless supply of milk and honey. This repeating tends to become habit forming.

Our repeated actions have some decreasing satisfaction, which leads to an additional type of what we can call dis-ease. We have the discomfort of the thing that upset us in the first place. Then we find that the out-there fix is temporary and we become upset again. The new frustration is caused by the fact that the out-there satisfaction is, by its very nature, fleeting. That tends to sour life and keep us stuck in places we don't enjoy.

Through the course of my work as an addiction clinician and spiritual counselor, I have discovered definite patterns in the common gratification-seeking behaviors of the people with whom I have worked. I also discovered some very important tools used by people who seek real results that are lasting. Many of them pay keen attention to that which is *within* their very being. These people find certain ways of *being* that tend to tap into the natural qualities found within themselves. These often-hidden satisfiers include love, joy, and peace. Many consider these sought-after states of mind as God qualities. People with this type of comfort-seeking somehow know that real satisfaction is not found in food, spirits, money, possessions, relationships, and other dissolving life-sweeteners.

To better visualize this out-there versus inner qualities concept, refer to the Life Source illustration. It shows three basic source types as represented by a Sun. The rays of the Sun are the out-there aspects of our outer self—the place of our everyday experiences. The Sun itself represents the Inner Self, which is our True Essence and is where we can find lasting gratification. The atmosphere area, or outer ring of the Sun, represents what I call the Bridging Tools—the actions we can take to change the traditional enjoyment-seeking out-there into actions that seek and find comfort from within. Refer to the Life Source illustration as we take a closer look.

Out-There Sources

The Sun rays section represents our outer self, or the human experience part of life. In it are the "doing" actions that are temporary quenchers. These are seen in the terms that are illustrated in the Sun's rays. Included in those rays are many manifestations of what our doing actions create: labels, roles, images, material possessions, failures, successes, boundaries, limitations, regrets, anger, fear, confusion, emotions, feelings, learning, and teaching. It is a mixed bag of ego things we might find positive or negative.

Also found in the out-there sun's rays are the human aspects of our experiences: peers, family, strangers, race, body, culture, senses, perceptions, expectations, judgments, worry, planning, personal character, personality, attitudes, thoughts, beliefs, life stories, physical gender, and sexuality. Likewise, it has our unawareness states of mind and free will. These human aspects are not good or bad—they just are. Critical to our understanding is knowing that their nature is to change. Even though we spend lots of time looking, and finding solace in these things, they do help us create some pretty uncomfortable conditions in life, as well. These out-there aspects of humanity do not permanently put our mind at ease no matter how long or how well we try.

Inner Self Source

The Sun part of the illustration details our Inner Self. It is our "spark of life," True Self, Higher Self, or God aspects. The labels shown include internal conditions that are rewarding by their very nature. Besides the primary source of all things (what many call God) is the vehicle by which creative qualities exist—Mind. More fully explained in Chapter Three, the Mind, ours and God's, is the source of Peace, Love, Truth, Faith, Consciousness, and Joy. Taken together, it is our Authentic Being Self. This inner place is where perpetual gratification is found even though this place is not very often where people look. It is important to note that any and all of us can understand the way in which we can tap into those qualities. We just have to know some secrets.

The Bridging Tools

Looking back to the "Life Source," I refer to the atmospheric ring found around the Sun labeled as Bridging Tools. They are grouped together in four categories: Our Innate Prompts, Mental Actions, Emotional Actions, and Being Actions. Bridging the outer self with the Inner Self, these action tools are some of the key ways we move our attention from *seeking* temporary fixes out-there to finding true inner comfort in our Higher Self.

First and most basic of all the tools is our direct line between spirit (inner spark of life) and the out-there aspects of thoughts and emotions. They are known as Intuition and Instinct. These natural and innate prompts in life can, if we pay attention, override the fear-based ego/self. Being mindful and aware of the importance of intuition and instinct propels us to not only listen to these inner inspirations, but also to act on their messages.

The beauty of intuition and instinct is that they are never fear-based. When we get a gut feeling and we are not sure if we should follow its message, we can simply ask, "Is this idea based on fear?" If it is based on fear, then it is not from your Higher Self, it is from your fear-based ego. Decisions based on fear never go well for long. Choose love-based Inner Self messages that surface from your gut—Instincts and Intuition.

The Mental Actions are the use of thoughts, prayer, visualization, affirmations, mindfulness, and meditation. These mind-related tools open the door for and create opportunities for going within.

The third category has the Emotional Actions: love, gratitude, forgiveness, and compassion. These four emotion-based tools create powerful energies for change.

The fourth category has the Being Actions. These states of "being" are: being love, being kindness, being authentic, and being open-minded. "Being" can be thought of as the truest form of what you call your life. These "Being" actions, therefore, solidify the pleasurableness that you find within—in the Inner Self place.

Imposter Comfort

Even if we discover that the true comforting energies are within us, we often fail to seek them. This is so because these gems are covered up by unsound thinking and beliefs about ourselves and about life in general.

Lilly's Story

Take, for example, the life of Lilly. When she learned that she was adopted by the people she knew as her parents, Lilly was more than disturbed. As a small child she always thought that being adopted was somehow unacceptable and "less than" when compared to the other children who were born into a family. When she discovered that she herself had been adopted, she felt a sudden lack of love.

As she entered adolescence, she came to believe that her parents viewed her as a possession—not a beloved child of their own. Possessions became a theme in Lilly's life. When she became a gainfully employed young woman, she started buying a lot of things that she did not need. As Lilly grew into adulthood, she used home shopping TV and later online shopping, spending endless hours searching. She found certain sweetness in shopping, buying, and having.

In the beginning, she would hide her purchases in the attic. The attic items were discovered by her husband, who was more than upset about the unneeded storehouse. In secret, Lilly then rented a storage unit that filled up in no time. Upon Lilly's death, it was discovered that she had four storage units full of merchandise that she never used. Buying and possessing was somehow false comfort for her irrational beliefs about her self-worth.

Like Lilly, we become convinced that we don't have love, peace, worthiness, and joy. So, we keep looking out-there. And why not, since so many things do provide a quick fix. But are we willing to pay the price? If you are reading this book, you probably are tired of chasing shallow fixes.

Review Points

We all have inner power—the same powers as our Creator.

- Implementation of knowledge as found in *The Kybalion* principles is a master's way to happiness.
- From the study of *The Kybalion* we learn it is a great source for ending pursuits of comfort-seeking as it leads us to inner comfort finding.

- Lasting and meaningful satisfaction from the upsets of life is found within our own being; it is not found in the endless number of temporary comforters found outside ourselves.
- Besides the inner and outer being aspects of our lives, we have bridging tools that help lead us from the outer to the inner.

Affirmations of Intention

I affirm that I live a life of more being—less doing.

I look inward for that which satisfies on a true level.

CHAPTER TWO

Being Busy

*I*t has been proved to me that it is always better to confront challenges with a good understanding of that challenge's nature. For that reason, it seems appropriate to look more closely at how our desires for pleasure and contentment work before we get into the seven principles themselves.

We have three basic levels of comfort-seeking behavior that are related to seeking "out there." These three stages are not distinctive and have no real lines of division. I divide them here for explanation purposes only. In reality, one blends into the other as the energy levels blur the lines away. They are:

- Survival Comfort-seeking
- Distraction Comfort-seeking
- Automatic Comfort-seeking

All three have important common characteristics. The seeking nature of them includes the fact that we are shopping for adjusters, refreshers, rewarders, and restoration fixes. As you can see in the Sun's rays of the Life Source illustration, the many outer aspects of life are about being driven by our human needs to seek satisfaction in the outer world of people, places, and things.

These three types of comfort-seeking actions are in contrast to finding true inner comfort, which is that process of finding natural inner well-being. By focusing our energies inward, and using natural tools to do so, we have a real chance at uncovering lasting inner comfort. Learning how to recognize the character of these out-there degrees of satisfaction assists in making more helpful choices in life. Let's take a closer look.

Survival Comfort-seeking

From having our diapers changed to satisfying hunger, we seek comfort for whatever our bodies, minds, and souls dictate. Most of these actions protect us, shield us, or otherwise make for our existence. Survival Comfort-seeking seems pretty natural and ultimately essential; for humans this a very pronounced aspect of life. People seek warmth from the cold, coolness in the heat. Although we enjoy our alone times, we seek the pleasure and warmth of friends and family in times of joy, sorrow, and play. It creates a life with more productivity, satisfaction, love, longevity; and all the while it feels good. For people, this is survival. Natural as all this is, something troublesome nonetheless creeps into the human experience.

Distraction Comfort-seeking

It does not take long for us to learn that if we are in emotional pain we can take our minds off the pain with distractions. Perhaps the distraction is eating a lot of what we find tasty, watching a marathon of TV shows, endless flipping through social media, or maybe playing a video game over and over just to win that next game.

There are romantic embraces and one-night stands. Sports have become a billion-dollar business as an exciting distraction from everyday life and it has become everyday life for many. The list of distractions is endless and most of them are harmless—in moderation. Some distraction behaviors, however, have the potential to become problematic because moderation loses its ability to reward for long.

Automatic Comfort-seeking

As one would expect, this might lead to habit-forming and mindless distractions that morph the energy into an automatic mode. Distractions that start to become obsessive are ways we get ourselves into real trouble. Almost any distraction behavior can reach higher intensity and greater frequency while acquiring emotion-charged urgency. The amount of time and energy spent in trying to achieve that form of comfort begins to interfere with our lives, becoming a burden itself.

While the repeated efforts become ingrained in our minds and bodies we develop a tolerance. With the tolerance comes dissatisfaction with the old requirements. We need more of the same or something new to satisfy. This new upset is distressing, thus triggering the demanding desire for more of the things from out-there; things that no longer put us at ease. We pursue them anyway because we believe this pursuit might satisfy us since it once did. This is the nature of how Distraction Comfort-seeking becomes problematic and automatic.

Certain external chemicals and internal sensations have addictive characteristics of their own. Tolerance is becoming dissatisfied with an external and temporary nice feeling. Selective foods impact the brain and body chemistry differently than others. Fatty, salty, and sweet foods have a satisfaction level that is so great they are used as key ingredients in "comfort foods." At some point we eat for pleasure instead of nutrition in an automatic way. Either way, our mindless or conscious automatic pursuits have the tendency to take over our sound thinking. It is an ego-driven behavior at this point.

Dean's Story

One example of Automatic Comfort-seeking is found in Dean's life. Dean was not an active child. His parents saw him as lethargic. He preferred video games over sports. He got a steady supply of messages from others that he was nerdy, geeky, and undesirable. He came to believe that he was, indeed, unacceptable. Dean made no effort to change his image and, in fact, sought more time with video games and less time with people. It comforted him on two levels. One was that he did not have to be around people that reminded him that he was unacceptable. Second, he occupied his free time endlessly with superficial but harmless fun and challenges.

The video games only satisfied to a certain degree. In time, Dean added mindless eating of snack foods while playing the games. Food and video games became a united activity that Dean could not imagine removing from his life. By the time Dean graduated from high school he was an isolated young man of 250 unhealthy pounds.

What of another type of hunger; when we feel empty on an emotional level inside? Some people say it feels as if they have a hole in their soul. After years of suffering with the feeling of emptiness, we might find a false sense of comfort in a bottle of alcohol or pills. It is easy for repeated use of those artificial and temporary satisfactions to become automatic abuse of those substances. And we may or may not care that some substances have physical and/or psychological addictive qualities in their very chemical nature.

Automatic Comfort-seeking is not limited to substances. We can become obsessed with gambling, sex, relationships, pornography, electronic games, social media, shopping—the list goes on. We become addicted to the pleasant feelings caused by the chemicals produced for us in our bodies as we engage in those activities.

Automatic Comforting That Is Addiction

Some Automatic Comfort-seeking is called addiction. When we are in physical or emotional pain we seek comfort. We often take being soothed beyond what is purposeful and therapeutic. We might start our pain reduction with ice. We soak, elevate, stretch, bandage, and otherwise treat our physical pains. Narcotics are powerful pain killers. They serve an important purpose in hospitals, where many procedures require some form of pain relief. People have learned, however, that if the pain-killing medication is good in the hospital, it can also be good in the home. The pleasing aspects of home bring even more sweetness. That narcotics are addictive in nature does not seem to bother most people until they or their loved ones become addicted to that medication. The American opiate addiction epidemic too often gets its start from simple pain management that became Automatic Comfort-seeking. It reaches a point where it is called addiction. This has led to an alarming number of opiate overdoses. For their own gain, pharmaceutical companies, hospitals, doctors, lawmakers, and drug dealers have learned to capitalize on this pain and to the addicts' avoidance of withdrawal sickness.

Bryan's Story

> A law-abiding citizen with not even a speeding ticket in his background, Bryan became incarcerated after being convicted of crimes related to breaking into small-town drug stores. In those break-ins, his sole focus was opiate-based drugs.
>
> Bryan's story of crime started with a car wreck that resulted in his being prescribed oxycodone. Bryan found the drug to have a pattern of easing pain only after it created a twenty-minute increase in pain. During the increase of pain, he frantically took more of the opiate. This unintentional misuse of the drug sometimes gave him a euphoric feeling that was extremely pleasant for Bryan. It did not take long for him to abuse the drug with deliberateness just because it felt good. This highly addictive drug took over Bryan's life.
>
> Feeding his addiction led to doctor shopping and later to breaking into drugstores. While he comforted himself with the idea that "It is not really that bad since it is just medication," in the end he was breaking into drugstores not to get high or kill pain—it was in order to avoid the sickness of withdrawal. A kind and decent man with no prior criminal background ended up spending nearly a decade in a state prison.

Thoughts and Beliefs

Another kind of Automatic Comfort-seeking has to do with our very thoughts, beliefs, and resulting behaviors that are unsound, irrational, self-deprecating, or negative in nature. At the top of the list of these tendencies is the notion that "I am not good enough" or "Something's missing in me." Beliefs such as these tend to make us seek out and find confirmations that our beliefs are correct. This type of Automatic Comfort-seeking is about being right. It is as if we are saying, "See, here is more evidence that I am not good enough—I couldn't even learn those dance steps." We don't like these beliefs, but we stay with them because they are familiar and therefore reassuring in a twisted sort of way. They become our "stories." Most of the time, we don't even remember we have the beliefs that perpetuate those stories.

Examples of the damage done by self-defeating beliefs are endless. Staying in an abusive relationship falls into this category. We know we should leave the relationship, but we stay because leaving would be scarier than staying with what is familiar. Not going to college because it might be too hard is another example. Finding fault in a string of lovers so that we have good reason to avoid commitment altogether is another. For all Automatic Comfort-seeking behaviors there reaches a point where we realize that there seems to be "never enough." And "never enough" makes us dis-eased.

True Inner Comfort

Reversing the direction of our efforts, then, is the path to take for finding the lasting and true satisfaction we seek. I discovered this notion many years ago in my own bumpy travels in life and in my work with patients and clients. Furthermore, I learned many important strategies for changing the direction of my seeking from out-there sources to actually finding satisfaction *inside* myself. These processes helped me "be" me and feel mentally at ease. The new tools allowed me to reduce the endless "doing" that was based on seeking gratification in people, places, and things. It let my fear-based ego settle down.

Approaches to living that create a "being" state rather than a "doing" one is about finding true inner comfort. Of course, while in a "being" state we end up doing things, but only as a result of *being*. This form of healthy "doing" results from living from the inside out.

Sometimes, looking inside seems counterintuitive. If we feel a lack of love, it only makes logical sense that we must not have any love. Therefore, seeking it outside ourselves in someone else seems the way to go. But love found in someone else is not satisfying when we are trying to take love from them. Eventually the love is exposed for what it really is—neediness. Even though we may feel a lack of love, it does not mean that we do not have love within our being. That lack feeling is based on an illusion. Love often is hidden under unsound beliefs that deny that it is there. Revealing the truth that love is part of our being allows us the opportunity to experience the feeling of love in ourselves, for ourselves, and ultimately for others—amazing if we only know to look inward.

Another look at the Life Source illustration reveals the Bridging Tools we can use for moving from our outer human experiences and reaching the inner pleasant qualities that are found inside. These are the tools and bridges we use to connect the out-there world to the *inner*. As found in the diagram, the tools are the key ways for changing direction and revealing those ever-present God qualities of peace, joy, love, and compassion. Most of us do not put the powerful tools of prayer, meditation, and the other bridging to use for the purpose of looking within. In fact, most people use many of these strategies to help achieve the outer world elements. This is a "doing" action that can be useful, but, as we have learned, not with lasting satisfaction.

The mental imagery of the Life Source illustration helped cement the concepts of inner me and outer world experiences. It was very helpful in dealing with my daily life issues. But during the heat of some drama I would all too often forget what I had learned. I would fail to recall my inner True Essences of love, joy, and peace. In a pain of some type I would suddenly find myself looking out-there for satisfaction. Then I became frustrated before remembering—oh yeah, it's not out-there, it's found inside. The concepts of the Life Source illustration would then pop back into my awareness and give satisfaction. At these times, I would ask myself, "How do I avoid these lapses in awareness?" The answer arrived in due time and it came in the unexpected form known as *The Kybalion*.

Review Points

- Comfort-seeking is natural and expected.
- We have choices in how to find satisfaction.
- Finding true inner comfort is about looking within.
- Maintaining true inner comfort is about more being, less doing.

Affirmative Prayer of Intention

I accept that there is but one Source of all.

I know that my essence is one with that Source.

I affirm my intention to be in harmony with the energies of the highest levels of life's qualities.

I deny that outer-world qualities have any power over me and I release any thoughts that distract me from my inner True Essence.

I am grateful for all that I have and for the ability to create according to my beliefs.

May my beliefs be those that are life affirming.

It is so.

And so, it is.

CHAPTER THREE

Being Mind

*E*verything in life begins with our mental power and a term called Mental Transmutation. This delves into the process of changing and transforming our own mental states and conditions. I see this process as the nature of God. Others may see it as a process of nature. Understanding how the Source of our being works is an important process when we consider that our Source's nature is our own nature.

The foundational aspect of the seven principles is the first one, the **Principle of Mentalism**. The Principle of Mentalism is the center of *The Kybalion* understanding and is about Mental Transmutation, which seems similar to science fiction at first glance. The other six principles basically stem from the first one like spokes from the hub of a wheel.

The Principle of Mentalism embodies the truth that "All is Mind." It is represented in the Inner Self part of the Life Source illustration.

"The All is Mind. The Universe is Mental.
—THE KYBALION

This principle tells us that there is a power that fuels a constant creative process. This power is known as "The All" with a capital T throughout *The Kybalion*. It is eternal, infinite, and immortal and is known as the Life Force or as I use it, Life Source. We can call it the Higher Power. We can consider "The All" to be Spirit. It is also the thing that is in our bodies, our surroundings, and, indeed, the Universe. It is this quality that results in the saying, "There is no spot where God is not." This says that "The All" is not limited to the "bearded man in the sky" image to which many of us were introduced as children.

The All is Mind. This is one of the more difficult understandings of this principle, and it is essential. We have been raised to think of our mind as somehow connected to our brain, and that means it is individualized for each person and therefore limited and small. Far from that, we are informed to see that Mind *is* God. Accepting that idea expands our understanding that what we have always seen as an individual mind within each person is actually one Mind; a Mind that is everywhere. This is the ultimate basis for the notion of Oneness. We appear as having a mind of our own, but the energies of each are connected; they are One, or, more accurately, It *is* One.

A simple illustration of this Oneness idea is seen when we use the analogy of God as represented with water. Imagine a container of water and the water is God. If we pour the water to an ice cube tray, it begins to have individualization within each cubicle. When we freeze the water-filled ice cube tray, we then have a new form of individualized water—ice cubes that in our analogy would be our individual selves and minds. In this simple representation, we are the solid form of our Creator. That one container of water (God) created separate individual cubes that no longer look like one, but they are One. When the trays of ice are left out to melt they can be poured back into the container and be as they were in the beginning—one container of water. This is the nature of Oneness and of The All. This is a remembering of who we are as a whole, one Mind.

The Three Initiates state: **"While all is in The All, it is equally true that The All is in All . . . Mind (as well as metal and elements) may be transmuted, from state to state; degree to degree; condition to condition; vibration to vibration. True Hermetic Transmutation is a Mental Art."**

The Universe *is in* The All. The Universe *is not* The All. Yet, The All is in the Universe. It's like this: *The All*, which is The Mind, is the container *and* contents of the Universe. The Mind is the vessel for the Universe and everything that is in it. Said in more common terms; the Universe *is in* God. The Universe *is not* God. Yet God is in the Universe.

When we look at The All we see that it is infinite, absolute, eternal, and unchangeable. The All is not changeable since the Mind (God) is absolute, infinite, and eternal. This absolute quality has the ramification of saying, "In mind, in The All, everything already exists. The All is therefore not in the realm of change." The universe is, however, the ever-changing contents of The Mind, of The All. And this is where we as human beings live—an adjusting place; an ever-evolving condition. This is the out-there aspect of life. It is where our experiences are. It is full of movement and transformation. Refer to the Life Source diagram.

The Principle of Mentalism promotes the notion that only change itself is permanent. Everything is continuously growing, moving, expanding, contracting, and otherwise mutating. This lack of permanence is not comfortable. People don't like all this shifting around. We don't like the furniture being moved about unless we are the ones moving the pieces where we want them. Most of us fear altered people, places, and things. Our ego-self exists primarily to protect us from the fears we have related to change. Our egos want to run our lives and often do. Mind is not ego; it is the opposite of ego. Since my focus is on laying a foundation for finding true inner comfort, I must stress that our desire for reassurance and fixing will go away to the degree we quit resisting change.

The important thing is that if we accept change as fundamental to life, then we may stop resisting change. Resistance to change leads to all types of discomfort. Going with the flow has its rewards.

Donovan's Story

To better understand how change in life often impacts most lives, let's take a look at Donovan. As a child in elementary school, Donovan was well-liked and popular. He felt mostly okay about his life. He easily made things comfortable for himself. Life was good. He used his mind in healthy ways and his ego minimally took charge.

One day his parents announced that the family was moving to another town. In short order, Donovan found himself ripped from his suburban life with a solid standing at a large school. He entered a somewhat rural home that was isolated. The students of the new and much smaller school had no interest in welcoming the new kid. This barring from the group felt like the worst form of rejection to Donovan.

Donovan was overcome with fear and acquired a strong desire to avoid any new things in life. He developed a serious case of depression that further ostracized him since he made no effort to connect with others. Instead, he started reading novels and purposefully distracted himself. He settled into a very uneasy state of living that was punctuated by a belief that he was not good enough, and that the only way to make life bearable was to control what little he could. This was his ego at work.

Resisting change became the primary energy of Donovan's life. Donovan spent long hours at the new town's public library. His thinking was negative from the start of each day and lasted the entire day—with the only outlet being the reading of novels—an escape that was comforting not only because it was within his control, but also, because it was a great distraction as he tried to live life through fictitious characters of a make-believe story. One story led to another in what seemed like a never-ending story of its own.

As with most of us, Donovan did not know that he had the power within his own thinking to alter how he felt. He came to believe he had no love, peace, or joy within him. He did not know the power of his mind. Through his limiting energy, he attracted what he feared the most—being outcast and unacceptable. Donovan would have benefited from knowing the importance of accepting change as fundamental to life. His ego would have been put in its place. Donovan would have naturally reconnected with his inner joy and let go of his out-there temporary satisfactions.

What Can Be Changed Is Our Thinking

Another important aspect of the Mentalist principle is the idea that The All creates with its Mind. This is the mental transmutation aspect of the Principle of Mentalism. We can change our minds by altering our thinking at our own will. We, as part of The All, can revise what we create by amending the perceptions of our minds— even reworking our desires, intentions, and goals.

It is not about changing the things in life that we don't like; it is about changing our perceptions of those things. That makes it a mental exercise.

This is significant because it gives us the opportunity to create from within rather than from the many "doing" activities out-there—such as Donovan's escape into books. He kept "doing" by reading. He perceived himself as unacceptable even though there were plenty of signs that he *was* acceptable. He would have benefited from some changes in his perception.

When we are uneasy with something in life and it is getting us down, we may be tempted to go home and indulge in tasty food just to feel better; or in Donovan's case, hide in his room, buried in a book. What most of us don't realize is that we have the power to change our minds, to alter how we are feeling and how we perceive. We can do this with our own will to do so. After all, we are the creators of our own stories.

Had Donovan been encouraged to do so, he may have enjoyed his new life. As it was, he did not. His life was evolving and Donovan had no control of much of it. Donovan had no awareness of the nature of how things in life evolve and how they can be perceived differently with new thoughts.

All Is Becoming, Nothing Is

This brings us to another "change" aspect of the Principle of Mentalism. Simply put, nothing is. All is becoming. This is a step further up in our understanding of the predictability of evolution. It makes sense that if everything is changing, then nothing is permanent. As a result, we really cannot truthfully say that this *is* this—as if it is this forever. It is, for this moment, what it is, but in the next space of time it is changed to something else—something newly evolved. Sometimes what it is now is dramatically altered. Sometimes the change is so subtle that we don't even notice it. All things evolve and are in movement. They are now this, and then they evolve into that. Life is inflow and outflow, birth and death, creation and destruction, a creative evolution of movement that gives birth to something newly made, but not really new.

> *Know that "this too shall pass." This is an acknowledgment that whatever is, is about to change: so, there is no reason to stress, worry, or otherwise panic. Let it change. Let it be. This is to say let it change—unless you plan to alter it yourself: accepting the consequences that surface.*

Consider this paradox as related to evolutionary change: Nothing is new in the sense that nothing could never have not existed before. Yet, everything is new in the sense that it was never quite like this before. Nothing can evolve from nothing; it evolves from that which was before. If I say "I am" with the understanding that "I am" is changing at all times, then I pass into something new at all times. The frequently used statement in recovery circles, "This too shall pass," is the recognition that all things are becoming even as we say that those things "are." So, nothing *is*—and all is *becoming*.

The Principle of Mentalism ideas further explain the nature of the ongoing change as relating to the existence of vibration. Vibration exists in all things and varies from thing to thing. This is the now commonly held scientific truism that all is energy. We will be looking into that much more in later chapters.

Regarding Donovan's situation, his parents acknowledged his changed energy and found counseling for him. They noticed that over time he did, in fact, learn to accept certain uncomfortable truths, which predictably led to comfort. He learned that resistance to most change is futile. His need for his overactive ego was greatly reduced. His Mind, with a capital M, did its natural thing—allowing Donovan to experience the love, peace, and joy found within—new vibrations. For all the Donovans out there, know that there is great satisfaction in accepting that change is a given. Find solace in what you can change by adjusting your perception, and know that the good, the bad, and the cherished in life are indeed always transforming.

Review Points

- We accept change as fundamental to life and stop resisting it.
- We know that we are a part of the process of transformation by way of our minds; we have the power to change our minds and feelings by refreshing our perception in a conscious manner.
- We acknowledge and take comfort in knowing that nothing really is because everything is becoming, so we know that "this too shall pass."

Affirmative Prayer for Acceptance

I embrace the awareness that there is but one Mind with many individualized expressions; there is One Source with many outlets.

As a fully connected and empowered mental source of energy, I am one of those expressions mentally, physically, and spiritually.

I use my mind consciously, not to change things, but to change my perceptions, meanings, and beliefs about those things I have no ability to change.

Transmutation of mind is my tool for creating a more harmonious life; a life of peace, joy, and love.

I accept change as a simple part of life and look for the good in all things. With this perception of good, I feel grateful for this evolutionary truth.

I release my attachments to the familiar as I embrace the refreshed, mold the evolved, and mentally work with that which is becoming.

I know these truths are within the nature of all things.

It is so, and so it is. Amen.

CHAPTER FOUR
Being In The All

Stemming from the Principle of Mentalism is the **Principle of Correspondence**. It presents the notion that there are three primary "planes" of vibration in the Universe; and there is always a correspondence between the Laws of Nature of the various planes. These planes are described as Physical, Mental, and Spiritual.

This teaching says that the only difference between Physical, Mental, and Spiritual qualities is the vibration rate. Today, science accepts that all things are energy and vibrate; each thing with its own signature of vibration. When *The Kybalion* was first spoken, these notions were not a part of science, just a part of spiritual teachings that sometimes predicted science discovery. Science now embraces these notions which create an exciting marriage of science and spirituality.

The Principle of Correspondence states it in these words:

> "As above, so below; as below, so above."
> —THE KYBALION

Grasping the understanding of this principle gives us a way of explaining many unknown, unproven, even mysterious paradoxes found in Nature. There are planes beyond our true knowing, but when we apply the Principle of Correspondence to them we are able to understand much that would otherwise be unknowable to us. That awareness in itself can be reassuring.

This correspondence works universally as it manifests. It does so within the various planes of the material, mental, and spiritual universes. Knowledge of the Principle of Correspondence allows mankind to intelligently reason from the Laws of Nature. We can gain knowledge from that which we do know and apply it to that which we do not know. We know much of the physical world scientifically from knowledge gained from many generations. From that knowledge we can draw conclusions in the mental and spiritual worlds of which we know much less.

The notion of "As above, so below; as below, so above" means there is a cooperation, harmony, agreement, and correspondence between planes of vibration. As you will see, this is important to finding true inner comfort. *The Kybalion* plane labels are as follows:

- The Great Physical Plane
- The Great Mental Plane
- The Great Spiritual Plane

According to *The Kybalion* authors, these are arbitrary and artificial divisions; there is only a degree of vibration that extends from the highest vibrations to the lowest vibrations on a continuum.

The Physical Plane

The vibration rate of the physical plane is slowest. This explains how matter may appear solid and permanent at any given time. Besides easily identified matter (such as a rock or a bee), the physical plane includes ethereal substances which graduate by way of higher vibration. Let's break some of them down just to help clarify the distinctions.

The Great Physical Plane has subplanes that include solids, liquids, gases, radioactive waves, particles, and matter. It also comprises ethereal substances, which is the medium for the energy waves of heat, light, magnetism, electricity, gravity, cohesion, and chemical affinity. To my surprise, the Great Physical Plane includes Mental energies, such as telepathy. This understanding of the physical plane expanded my concept of what is physical.

The Mental Plane

Moving up in the degrees of vibration, the Mental Plane vibration has an even higher rate. As its name indicates, it includes mental aspects of life. We might immediately think of the brains of animals and humans. This principle broadens our concept of "mental" to include the mental aspects of mental mineral world, mental plant world, mental world of elements, mental animal world, and the mental human mind aspects. In increasingly higher rates of vibrations we have mineral thought force; plant intelligence; mental conditions of elements; animal instincts and thought; and human mind. The Great Mental Plane also has subplanes, including mineral mind—not the molecules, atom aspects—its soul; chemical mind—not the molecules, atom aspects—its soul; elemental mind—invisible intelligence of element beings; plant mind—having life, mind, souls; and human mind—which has its own complex subcategories. I present these categories for the purpose of showing all the complexities of the correspondence of all things. It is amazing if you think about it.

Consider that our understanding of what is mental is expanded to include all mental aspects of the universe. In this way we can understand how The All, which is Mind, is *in all things* and is so by its mental aspects as outlined above. It is fascinating to consider that on some very low vibration rate a rock has mental activity; certainly not in the same way that animals and humans or even plants do, but nonetheless the seemingly inactive rock has connection with vibrations of all else in the universe by way of mental energy. The rock, through its own individualized vibration, knows how to be a rock. Similarly, flowers and bees know how to run their life cycles through Mental energy. Not only does a bee know how to be a bee; it knows how to just be.

The Spiritual Plane

The Spiritual Plane includes *entities* about which we know the very least. They are beings whose life, mind, and form vibrate at the highest degrees. This understanding is not about the simple ideas of ghosts and the hereafter. These entities of the spiritual plane are the energies that help humans in the process of their evolution.

We can conclude that these energies are more evolved than humans, and they correspond with us with positive intentions. When I say positive intention, I must clarify by saying that some of the positive that comes from these entities may not seem so positive to us on our level of thinking; nonetheless, the intentions are life-affirming and therefore positive to evolution. In day-to-day life, we might have to take what seems as one step back in order to take what seems as two steps forward. Another is the idea that sometimes we enjoy an unexpected pleasure in life after experiencing uncomfortable events that were equally unexpected; yet they paved the way for that unexpected pleasure.

The Spiritual Plane subplanes have been given terms that we all have heard before, but none of them were termed "ghost" by the three initiate authors. Those anonymous authors put them in order of vibration rate as Human Avatars, Angels, Archangels, Ascended Masters, and Deities.

It goes almost without saying that if you fail to believe in such entities, then they will remain quiet in your human experience. *It is as you believe*—in your life. It is comforting to know that these entities exist for helping us, in cooperation with the Laws of Nature, in our evolution; and helping us in our times of need. It makes sense that these energies, by whatever names or terms you want to call them, are part of our existence and are here to assist us. We must take the time and expend the energy to engage with that energy if we want to benefit from these helpful spiritual forms.

Satisfaction Related to Correspondence

We just covered the structure of the three planes of vibration with its billions of degrees of movement. What does it mean to our quest for finding true inner comfort? Let's reflect on the very foundation of the Principle of Correspondence: "As above, so below; as below, so above" relates to the vibration levels of all things Physical, Mental, and Spiritual. Simply put, what is true in the Physical scientific realm is also true in the Mental realm, which is also true in the Spiritual realm. It runs up and down the vibration spectrum.

Is it not gratifying to know that the aspects of Spirit are found in us physically and mentally too? Such Divine aspects as faith (a belief that something greater than our human selves is available to soothe us), compassion, love, peace, joy, and comfort are ever-present—they are indeed in our spiritual realm, in our lower vibration selves, which includes our mental and physical selves.

> *All the good is already in us. We just have to permit the hidden characteristics and resulting pleasures to surface.*

In more traditional terms, we as humans are formed in our Creator's image. This is a more understandable way of seeing that the good of life—the parts of life that are unchanging, such as love, peace, and joy—are hardwired into us. Although these qualities frequently are hidden, love, peace, and joy will manifest in different ways at different times. The bottom line is that these heaven-like characteristics of Nature exist in us always and are in fact the things of our very essence. This is a different understanding of who we are, what we are.

On the other hand, day-to-day living and our ongoing challenges in life somehow give the feeling that these qualities are missing. In life, we spend a lot of time and effort looking for those true essence qualities and find them in temporary forms "out there." Consider this: Everything already exists, so the lower vibrations of love progressively look less and less as love as the vibration lowers. At some point, as the rate decreases, we stop calling these lower vibrations love and judge them negatively with the terms of fear or hate.

Many sages over the generations have said that hate and fear only exist in our own minds. The Principle of Correspondence lets us know that through vibration, the energy of love is what is real; hate and fear are simply terms we use for the lowest vibrations of love. They are our judgmental labels.

These negative judgments take on their own meanings and we start seeing them as real and separate from love. We must keep in mind that the various vibrations are not separate at all. That notion allows us, then, to use transformation, transmutation, and transcendence to experience the higher vibrations. In these ways we can purposely experience the love vibration on the higher levels, which are more as we enjoy it. This is where use of our mind comes in.

Original Sin—Fact or Fiction?

Taking another cue from the notion that rewarding states already exist within us allows us to see another aspect of "As above, so below; as below, so above."

We have all heard of the idea that humans are born with "original sin." This is a disheartening idea. A more literal explanation of this religious and sometimes cultural idea is that humans are born with the ability to "miss the mark," which is the meaning for the word *sin* in its original use. This ancient archery term has taken on its own life in some religions and seems to damn everyone right from the start. Many of us are taught from the very beginning that we are supposed to miss the mark; so, we all are sinners. It is as if none of us has a chance to escape ongoing mistakes, poor judgments, and bad behavior. It is no wonder that we feel the need for being saved by something out-there.

The Principle of Correspondence, however, puts a cleaner spin on this notion of original sin. From a vibration standpoint we can see that lower vibrations already exist in us (original). At the very lowest vibrations we may view our feelings, expressions, and manifestations as sin.

Using the example of love again, love exists in us when we are born (original) and so do its corresponding lower vibrations that humans have judgmentally labeled as fear and hate. It is more accurate to say we have love in our Nature to varying degrees of vibration—including those at the lower energy rates that have been considered sinful ones—such as hate and fear. Transforming, transmuting, and transcending are ways to get "saved" from those lower vibrations.

The Question of Heaven and Hell

Many of us are attracted, like moths to a light, to the brightness of a place called heaven. The disconcerting and age-old question as to where heaven exists is resolved in the quote: "As above, so below: as below, so above." While it seems that many religious teachings have tended to locate heaven as above us in outer space somewhere, Biblical statements contradict that location reference and say that it is "at hand." This may not be an either/or issue as many religious scholars have debated.

With the notion "As above, so below" we realize that what we call heaven is actually located both above Earth and on Earth. Granted, we have the choice to perceive it as in one place or the other. Perhaps most of the peoples of the earth have such duality thinking. Duality is a troubling and troublemaking point of view which will be discussed in depth later. The True Essence qualities of love, peace, and joy are conditions that we do experience on Earth and we are told that they are promised to us in Heaven. A lot of people spend much uncomfortable time preoccupied with this idea.

The Principle of Correspondence lets us know that these higher vibrations exist physically, mentally, and spiritually. This is a huge departure of common understanding about where the qualities known as heaven are, and it is profoundly comforting. It stands to reason that the inner qualities that would make up the elements of Heaven do exist on all three planes, Physical (on Earth), Mental (our perceptions), and Spiritual (beyond the limits of physical and mental life).

A Look at Below

Some people are less motivated by the light and more motivated to avoid the heat of consequences. From an anxious place, they are preoccupied with avoiding hell (or jail, or other negative consequences) even if they don't make it to heaven. "As above, so below; as below, so above" calls into question the existence and location of hell in the same manner as heaven. The same line of thinking related to heaven would also apply to the notion of hell since the lower vibrations exist on all three planes.

Heaven and hell exist everywhere as conditions at all times. The one we experience depends on the vibration rate of that which we focus upon the most. The higher and more positive our vibration is, the more heavenly—the more God-like.

It is pretty easy to perceive hellish qualities on Earth in the physical aspects of life. We can perceive the lower vibrations in mind. We have the option to allow the lower vibrations to mandate our awareness of the hellish conditions that we term fear, hate, distrust, pain, and anguish. While the vibration rates dictate as to whether any specific aspect of life is physical, mental, or spiritual, what is true is that there is a correspondence between what is found below and what is also found above. This correspondence helps us understand the Nature of both heaven and hell as existing on three planes. We can understand the Nature of heaven and hell from our daily Earthbound experiences.

We can conclude, then, that heaven and hell do not really exist as a couple of locations; they simply are terms for higher and lower vibrations that exist throughout the universe in Physical, Mental, and Spiritual planes.

When we are seeking feelings of well-being for one thing or another in life, we can ask, "Are we focused on the higher energies of love, peace, and joy; or are we focused on the feelings and perceptions of lesser amounts of love, peace, and joy—conditions that are commonly stated as hate, fear, unrest, and anguish?" It is our choice.

It is worth repeating that only the Divine qualities truly exist. Love, peace, and joy are ever-present. However, by the construct of duality, we have come up with the terms hate, fear, and anguish to express our discomfort with those qualities on lower vibrations. The truth is that they are really just uncomfortable states of (less love, less peace, and less joy) vibrations. When we remove the duality aspect of our perceptions and use polarity aspects of varying degrees, we find that heaven and hell are simply labels for that which we enjoy and that which we do not. There is unconditional love at the top of the pole and hellish fear at the bottom of the pole. That being said, there is nothing wrong with the idea of heaven being above and hell being below—especially if we use the image of a metaphoric pole of vibration.

Considering that love, peace, joy, and all other God qualities are found within us—not just out-there—we can see that comfort from the lower vibrations truly is an inside job. We find security in knowing all the good is already in us. When we do this, our ego has no need to protect us, no need to pull us to the out-there comforts.

With egos and fear in check, we can live from the inner fountain of our being. We can do the things that inspire and energize ourselves. We can choose to serve those values that make us lose the sense of time and space and fatigue. If we choose to not be concerned with opulence, status, duty, and other ego-driven ideas, we get a chance to follow our bliss. In this way we achieve the comfort of serenity.

Bliss is bound to happen if we follow the wishes of our Higher Selves instead of the wishes of our egos. How can our Higher Selves not direct each of us to our highest good and a joyful state of well-being? In turn, this will automatically include our personal experience as being harmonious, loving, and wise as a corresponding outcome. How would our lives be different if we routinely went about our affairs with a consciousness of our place in the universe? Wouldn't our feelings and our deeds be different than if we continued to go about our "doing" and our out-there styled lives?

Reflect on this gratifying notion: Everything is filled with Divine Spirit. We are aspects of Divine Energy. All our thoughts reflect Divine Thought. All our thoughts come from Divine Mind. We can ask if our thoughts are worthy of the Divine Mind within each of us. From here, all desires are a manifestation of Divine Desire. All our desires are driven by Divine Desire to experience life fully. We can learn to make every desire reflect our highest goals. What is worth achieving here is to always do our best in thought and action so that

Divine is reflected in the physical and mental planes of life, as well. Ego is not necessary.

Odela's Story

The story of Odela shows how failure to use the ideas found in the Principle of Correspondence creates discomfort.

By the time Odela was in high school her tendency to be neat and orderly was well established. She had become a perfectionist. She worked very hard to get the A grades.

College academics were easier than high school for Odela because she listened to her ego and avoided courses she felt would be too hard. She found people that were equally motivated for high grades and set up study groups with them. The study groups led to connections with a crowd of students who liked to party. Odela suddenly discovered the sweet sensation of free abandon. Alcohol gave her a temporary freedom from the stress she placed on herself for high achievement and perfection.

At the same time that she began partying, Odela also began feeling an urge for some sort of spiritual connection. As she "church shopped," she got baptized two more times because different denominations told her that the form of baptism she already had was not valid. All that was a form of perfectionism outpictured in her spiritual trek. She did not find spiritual peace in the out-there aspects of religion.

At a very low time of her life, Odela met a spiritual leader in her community. Through that relationship she discovered that all the good was already in her. She learned ways to transform and transcend barriers and uncover her hidden God qualities. Meditation, love, mindfulness, self-forgiveness, and gratitude-based prayer became her daily routines. She realized that she could not predict how much she would drink when it came to alcohol, so she abstained from alcohol 100 percent. Odela learned to live with the highest of intentions that she could find.

With her new-found perceptions, those intentions did not require perfection, nor did the outcomes. Her ego focused on the fact that the out-there aspects of life were no longer in charge. Although she was not aware of it at the time, she was focused on raising the vibrations of her life.

Just as was true for Odela, having a clearer picture of who we really are as beings is helpful in overcoming the demands made by our fear-based egos. Furthermore, without the ego energy's constant interference, we will experience the natural and inner beauty within us—love, peace, and joy. A basic understanding of the Principle of Correspondence on all planes certainly does help us in finding true inner comfort.

Review Points

- We can gain knowledge from that which we do know and apply it to that which we do not know. What we know of the physical world corresponds with the unknown mental and spiritual realms.
- In the spiritual realm it is comforting to realize that there are invisible entities to help us use the Laws of Nature in our evolution and that asking for that assistance does not go unnoticed.

- "As above, so below" correspondence helps us understand the Nature of heaven and hell as existing in our daily Earthbound experiences; heaven and hell are terms for higher and lower vibrations that exist throughout the universe in Physical, Mental, and Spiritual planes. We make our own heaven and hell in our living lives.
- There is satisfaction in knowing that good is already within us; and when we take responsibility in a conscious effort in life and do our best in thought and action, we thrive.

Affirmations for Higher Intentions

The following affirmations cover a number of ideas. Read through them in troubling times and the most effective one will stand out to you immediately. Some can become standard go-to statements in their present form or as altered by you to better fit your desires.

I affirm that I have the ability to increase vibration and therefore improve my life.

I affirm that my intentions are those that lead to my highest good and I tap into the spiritual energies and entities to improve my physical and mental energies.

I affirm a decision to lead my life consciously and purposefully with the intention to honor all living things as well as myself.

I affirm an inner joy that is achieved by seeing beyond lower vibration aspects of life; by knowing a greater Truth of my being.

I affirm that peace is found within my being and is not dictated by the many outer and worldly perceptions of contradictions and conflicts.

I affirm that I find harmony in life by personal acceptance of all aspects of life; being free of judgment and keeping the awareness that whatever is uncomfortable will change in one way or another.

I affirm I will not be fooled by appearances and I affirm that true to my Nature and the Nature of all things, there is abundance in life; more than I could ever fully consume. I welcome all that I see as good and I perceive all as good.

I affirm that, contrary to what I have been taught and hear around me, my very Nature is that of being, not doing. I do because I "be." Being is an inside place.

CHAPTER FIVE

Highest Being

Vibration is so central to all seven of the principles that it has already been presented quite a lot in this study. A look at the **Principle of Vibration** gives us a chance to go into real depth about the nature of vibration as it explains the idea that motion is found in everything in the Universe. There is real satisfaction in manipulating vibration. The principle states:

> "Nothing rests; everything moves; everything vibrates. Everything moves, vibrates, and circles."
> —THE KYBALION

It explains that *Mind* and *change* are the creative process by way of the energy known as vibration. The Principle of Vibration accepts that nothing is at rest—even if it appears so. This idea explains, as we have already learned, the differences between various manifestations of Matter, Mind, and Spirit; they are the result of different rates of vibration. In a literal sense, vibration is the quality that gives the distinctions in each of those planes.

Matter vibrates at the slowest rate. According to the principle, The All vibrates at the highest rate. Theoretically, if the molecules of matter vibrate faster and faster they would ultimately take the matter from the visible to the invisible realm.

God is at an infinite level of vibration, almost to the point of being at rest. You can think of this in the same way that the spokes of a bicycle's wheels seem to disappear by "magically" blurring to invisibility by the spinning speed. We can conclude that there are millions upon millions of varying degrees between the highest level, such as our Higher Power, and the objects of the lowest vibrations, such as rocks and paralyzing fear.

The higher vibration rates a person operates upon, the more pleasant the vibration he or she will experience. It is our choice as to what vibration we have and it is according to our focus. It is important to remember this in times when life feels uncomfortable.

Raising Vibrations

To change our mental state is to change vibration. To transform our dis-ease, we deliberately raise our vibration. As stated earlier, this is significant for the purpose of seeking some sort of release because the energy found in *temporary* comforts is found at the lower vibration rates. Referring to the Life Source illustration, these are the out-there things in the rays' section of the diagram. And the real satisfaction qualities of love, peace, and joy are found at *higher* vibration rates, which are illustrated in the Sun section of the Life Source. The Inner Self has a higher and satisfying energy.

For example, temporary low vibration is attached to our unpleasant feelings and can manifest that out-there lower vibration in the mindlessly eating of sugary foods. Likewise, we have the choice to find more permanent sweetness in the higher vibration of self-love, forgiveness, or peace. *We can raise the vibration rate by way of our will.* We can deliberately focus our attention upon a more desirable state, which is to say, we focus our attention on a different, higher vibration by willing it so. There are many ways to "will" it so and we will explore those later.

Where we put our emphasis in life is not only important to our individual lives, it works within our families, communities, and even on a global level as well. Addressing the energy of fear with more fear-based solutions just builds up more fear and negativity. Truly, the ills of the world are based on fear of one sort or another.

Positive focusing is a form of what we can call transformation. At its most extreme, this process can be called transmutation. It is transforming one aspect of life along its continuum of energy. It is a process of moving energy away from lower vibration to higher vibration; from distressing aspects to soothing desired aspects.

There are known and proven ways we can focus our attention. The simplest and primary way is to *think* about it repeatedly. Thinking is in the nature of Prayer. As a result, prayer acts as a powerful thinking tool. Visualization falls into the same category; as do Affirmations, Masterminding, and Meditation. These are the Bridging Tools illustrated in the Life Source diagram. Being aware of vibration and its power gives us the opportunity to take responsibility for what we create.

Focusing on the Negative

The catch here is that even if we fail to *consciously* focus our attention on whatever it is that we desire—such as self-love—in times of disturbances we tend to still put our attention on something, predictably the very thing that disturbs us. We manifest according to what we focus our attention upon deliberately or absentmindedly. The bottom line is we create and attract the things of whatever vibration rate we focus upon.

Let's take the example of mindlessly eating sugary foods to ease the pain of life. Focusing on any *lower* vibration, such as beliefs of lack and limitation, leads us to the lower vibration thoughts of self-loathing, low self-worth, and poor self-esteem. We will most certainly continue to be attracted to lower-vibration rate out-there items, such as ice cream. Lower-thought vibrations correspond to lower-vibration enjoyments.

Unbeknown to us, it is by way of vibration that we can, in an unintentional or mindless manner, create the very thing we do not desire—the thing from which we want to be free. We are essentially allowing our unhealthy "default" thinking of poor self-esteem, for example, to dictate a continuation and even regression of poor self-esteem and its accompanying search for sugary foods. You can substitute sugary foods with any number of other reliefs—such as alcohol, gambling, sex, medication, illicit drugs, video games, pornography, unhealthy relationships, internet, social media, running, electronic games, cleaning, shopping, work, and control—and the list goes on. It is our choice of focus that determines our manifestations.

If we want to have liberation from low self-worth, we consciously set the intention to focus on the higher qualities of self-love. This attracts dynamics and energies of life that help us experience and "vibrate" at higher rates. Our awareness and focus are forms of *healing* for the low self-worth we had in the first place. An example of this is found in Odela's journey, where she tried to overcome her feelings of low self-worth with perfectionism. Her healing was found in the higher vibrations of self-love as found within.

Blocked Vibration: Question Perceptions

What happens if our vibration is blocked? Blocking a vibration literally creates stress, lack of creativity, and a closed state of being. This can result in feelings of lack; lack of forgiveness, lost love, lower self-worth, less satisfaction, and other dis-eased states of mind. Unhealthy life conditions are created. These conditions naturally prompt us to take action that is often of the lower vibrations found in unhealthy temporary gratification—such as those sugary foods I keep mentioning or even more destructive out-there things.

There are countless causes for these blockages in life, but a few stand out as archetypal. The vast majority of them are the result of unsound, limiting, or irrational beliefs. These lower-vibration-rate beliefs can lock the door on the passage of the energy of vibration. A case of this could be in someone's belief that they are so low on the totem pole of life that they do not have the right, the ability, or the inner constitution to advance in life any further than they already are. This highly limiting life-path belief will tend to repeatedly be in charge of the person's life. The ego gets into action. It will hold the energies that could advance a person's life behind the locked door of opportunities. The energies and perceptions of the limiting belief don't even allow dreaming or planning for anything other than what the person already possesses in life. The energies of evolution and opportunity are blocked.

It all begins with a perception from whatever limiting source that we accept as true. From there, the meanings we give events in life all narrow down to acceptance of only those ideas that conform to the unsound perception. This, in turn, forms a commanding belief of which we are not fully aware: that belief runs the show, whether we are aware of it or not. We become the victim of our own hidden irrational beliefs. With this type of perception, most of the energies we potentially have for advancement in life are shut down.

It is important that we have the awareness that we can let go of whatever we are holding on to and therefore allow the stress and blocks of thinking to be free. We can learn to practice letting go when we discover that we have, for whatever misguided reason, grabbed on to and remained attached to something.

Letting Go

Knowing the nature of the Principle of Vibration allows us to see that we do have the ability to reverse that shut-down state. We can accept that vibration is ever-present in whatever form it takes in life. We can embrace the notion that we do not have to keep holding on to the energies of crippling beliefs. If the belief is not working for us, we can consciously *will* the change of it.

It has to be noted, however, that changing our perceptions is pretty difficult if we don't consciously let go of the thoughts and feelings upon which we are already clinging. We will not progress to a new vibration or allow the flow of energy if we are still holding on to that cherished old vibration. Knowing that the higher pulsation rate is a more restorative one, we should be pretty eager to take the first step in change. The first step is to *be willing* to let go of the current unhealthy perception and any related beliefs. The second step—we *let go*. It sounds simple and easy. It is a simple and straightforward notion; but in truth it is not so easy to accomplish.

The reason it is not trouble-free is that letting go of some things seems painful and scary. It is a fear-based change. The good news is that we are ideally only letting go of our attachments to the *perceptions and notions* we have of people, places, and things. It is not letting go of the people, places, and things themselves. The potential changes related to people, places, and things will happen (on its own) once the perception and vibrations change. Letting go, for our purposes here, is really about letting go of our *attachment* to certain perceptions. Releasing the need to have an old familiar perception is the goal. It is important to remember that old familiar views provide a comfort of their own even though we may be aware of its undesirable, hurtful outcomes.

Case in point: If my perception is that I am a *limited* person, *being limited* has taken over my life by way of an unsound belief that supports that perception. I lead my life in such a way that much of what I manifest confirms and conforms to that limiting belief. Odd as it may seem, it is distressing for me if things happen that could prove that I am in fact *not* a limited person. In a mindless manner, I reject any higher levels of vibration. It would seem that I prefer to accept that which is in alignment with my belief, even though the manifestations that come from that belief are

Consciously and deliberately letting go of the poison-belief gives us freedom to choose whatever we desire instead. Once our minds are free of the old, they are ready for the newly changed.

self-harming and painful. It is a case of hating our poison but liking its taste. It creates a self-fulfilling prophesy and keeps us stuck in life.

If I release my attachment to controlling my environment and other people's behavior, feelings, and attitudes, then I feel no suffering; anything that is not in alignment with my ideas of how things should be are no longer of concern. "Letting it go" is not about letting go of that which we don't like. It is not about keeping things from changing. It is not ridding our lives of troubling things. Instead, it is about changing the energy of holding on to something (and its vibration) that isn't life-affirming. It is about allowing energy to flow, and to flow to higher rates of vibration.

Letting God

We hear the statement "Let go and let God" a lot in the recovery and substance abuse treatment arena. The second part of that statement is a letting go process on a different level. It stands to reason that if we are letting go and allowing a higher rate of vibration, such as transforming self-loathing into self-love, we are tapping into another equally important aspect of self-directed change—letting our Higher Power.

> *To "Let God" is about allowing the very highest vibration, that of our Higher Power, which is found within, to correspond with us on all planes of our being—physical, mental, and spiritual. This is the meaning of the commonly heard statement, "Thy will be done."*

True to the notion that the very highest rates of vibration are those closer to the vibration of The All, we also have to consider *letting* Higher Power run the show. This type of "letting" is about being in alignment with the easier-flowing, nonconflicted energies found naturally all through the universe. We can see that letting our Higher Self is about allowing the natural tendency of evolution to align itself with higher vibration. Therefore, we experience more comforting conditions when we look within.

From a practical point of view, this understanding as a whole is what we call Divine Right Action. Our deductions related to finding true inner comfort are:

- "Letting it be" is the *acceptance* aspect of being.
- "Letting go" is the *liberation* aspect of movement.
- "Letting God" is *the highest way* of being and is found within.

There are real benefits to consciously letting God because allowing those quiet powers of love, peace, and joy is about embracing vibration in all ways; embracing those energies all of the time. It opens us to what true love is; opens us to what is becoming and evolving; connects us with awareness of God and Nature; sets us free; and allows for balances in our life circumstances. This allows a loving detachment from those things that are negative and those things that are positive, because even the positive is bound to change some day. It is living in Faith that something greater than our human selves is available to us. Letting love, peace, and joy be the vibration of choice brings us closer to higher states of life related to health, wealth, and creativity. It is *manifesting abundance*. This is the essence of true satisfaction.

Tools for Change

We can bridge the out-there aspects of our lives with the Inner Self aspects with a number of transformation tools. (You might want to again glance at the Bridging Tools part of the Life Source illustration at this point.) For our purposes of changes toward lasting gratification, I organized the tools into four general groups: *Innate*, *Mental*, *Emotional*, and *Being*. They have within them the energies that allow the light of inner qualities to shine within.

Innate Tools for Change

As already mentioned, Innate Actions are those that just simply come about naturally. These gut feelings are our intuitions and instincts. They spring out of our very innermost being but seem to come out of nowhere. We explain them as "I don't know how; I just know." And indeed, we do just know. As long as we listen and act from the love-based awareness, we are assured to have pleasant and healing manifestations. Sudden feelings of dread or anxiety, on the other hand, are not instincts or intuition—they are ego emotions based on fear. Some of these may help us survive a crisis, like outrunning a wolf. For resolving most day-to-day disturbances, we do far better by listening to our gut.

Mental Tools for Change

In the Mental realms are thoughts, prayer, visualization, affirmations, Masterminding, positive thinking, mindfulness, and meditation. These tools are related. They all deal with mental efforts to one degree and possess varying degrees of emotional charge. Let's take a closer look of each.

Thoughts
Casual and directed thinking that focuses on what is desired is essential. This thinking is critical for creating. Thoughts are things.

They are vibration and they impact things in their path. More intentional and action-oriented thinking includes such things as having dreams and hopes in life, setting goals, making plans, and taking small and large steps related to those products of thought. These are the thought energies of change.

Prayer

I often have seen how prayer seems to change recovering addicts' lives. Prayer is a form of directed, intentional thoughts possessing higher levels of vibration. Prayer is highly focused thought.

Prayer-related thoughts that are packaged through some form of formal structure, such as religion, can create a powerful focus. The power of prayer is intensified if the thinker or thinkers are also charged with emotions—which is often the case. Also, prayer stated aloud has more vibration than those said silently. And when two or more are gathered for prayer each thinker increases the energy and vibration of that prayer. Asking to be in alignment with God and prayers of gratitude are the most powerful forms of prayers and engage the Law of Attraction. Such is the nature of change by prayer.

Visualization

When we think of visualization we might consider it somewhat fanciful in nature. Maybe visualization seems like daydreaming and whimsical ideas. In truth, visualization is image-laden mental action. People who practice visualization reap the benefits of the higher octane found in thoughts that have the added energies of sight, sound, smell, touch, and even taste if the vision so includes them. Visualization done right is a smart and creative use of vibration.

FINDING TRUE INNER COMFORT

Affirmations

The use of affirmations has left the confines of spiritual circles and found its way into the practice arenas of sports, theater groups, business meetings, and even the everyday lives of enlightened exam-bound students and purpose-driven adults; and for good reason. Affirmations work.

Affirmations are products of our thoughts. Unlike random or emotion-based thoughts, affirmations are ideas presented and repeated by way of positive and intentional statements. Most of the time they are short and to the point so they can become mantras for business associates and for religious groups. They are often used as chants in the same way—especially for sporting teammates. An affirmation, properly constructed, has proved itself effective in directing a focus that is contagious, engaging, and habitual. The habit promotes a focus that allows the transformation of lower-vibration aspects of life into the higher-vibration aspects. If affirmations are stated aloud, they carry the added benefit of sound energy. *What all affirmations need for creating change is an emotional attachment to a positive and life-affirming intention as put to words.* Affirming the truth about your true being and your Inner Self is powerful.

Masterminding

With widespread popularity, Masterminding is a specific effort for outcomes done by a group of people for an *individual*. The basic process has been around for centuries, but it is believed to have been first defined in a formal way by Napoleon Hill in his 1920s book *The Law of Success*. There are lots of variations, but all are about identifying and focusing energy for the benefit of an individual who has a desire for change. The person at the center of the activity likely has a general idea of what they want to achieve and presents that to the other group members. Trusted group members settle into those ideas and allow a creative and inner connection to bubble up additional ideas from within.

The combining of energies is gathered specifically to assist evolution in a directed way. Someone who wants to expand the possibilities by way of the instincts, intuition, and the inner stirring of loved ones gives permission to express, in a sacred way, that which feels safe and enriching. The combined energies of Mastermind procedures have the tendency to tap into the inner selves of everyone in the group. This is so because it inclines the use of inner vibrational "being" avenues rather than thoughts alone or out-there notions.

Positive Thinking

Slightly different from Affirmations and Thought is what many refer to as positive thinking. It was made famous by Norman Vincent Peale in his book *The Power of Positive Thinking*. In its simplest form, it encourages us to mold our minds and speech to be positive in nature. It is about changing our *tendency* to think of the negative things we perceive, and instead be inclined to see the positive of it. Peale contends that there is always a positive way of perceiving everything—even the most distasteful of things.

Falling into this category is the idea that we can always learn from anything in life. Learning from unfortunate things of life is a positive. Another notion is that we can accept the idea that whatever we perceive is flawed. This is so because all perceptions are limited and therefore incomplete. In other words, there is more to the story and often a different version. Why be negative about something that is only partly known? One more aspect is the fact that nothing is really negative in and of itself; it is negative only because of our opinion and judgment. To be sure, we can change our opinion if we have the will and wisdom to do so. That is positive thinking.

Mindfulness and Meditation

Unlike the previous mental-action thought tools, the next bridge is not about the content of our thoughts. It is related to transmutation and elevation of mental activity, the Mind. With it, one state of being is fully altered into another state of being.

Called *mindfulness,* it is one of the highest, most effective tools for getting to that place we call "being," that place in the Life Source illustration known as Inner Self. It is reaching into our Higher Self. Mindfulness is basically being inclined to have awareness of one thing or another *in the present moment.* Mindful meditation and mindful living are matters of vibration management.

Practicing mindfulness is focusing our attention on the here and now. It takes our attention away from past regrets and pain. It takes our attention away from the future, where we spend time planning, projecting, and worrying. It puts our attention on the now moment that is neutral in judgment. In ways that are not fully understood, the practice of being mindful, whether in meditation or living, allows an elevation of vibration throughout our Physical, Mental, and Spiritual planes. With this solace, we realize that we have changed the very nature of our full being. This is called alchemy, or transmutation. For example, consider changing a form that has unintentionally become a human *doing* of depression into a human *being* of joyful expression.

How do we enact this mindfulness transmutation process? We stop past and future thinking and start present moment awareness.

It is a practice of mental discipline. We discipline ourselves to pause random monkey-mind thinking. In a very real sense, mindfulness is a continuation of *Letting God*. We use pauses in active thinking in order to transmute our overall state of being. We transmute from a status that is stressed, dis-eased, or otherwise upset into a state of being that is relaxed and at ease. We have raised our vibration to that which is akin to the vibration of love, peace, and joy.

We practice getting into the spaces between thoughts—where the vibration has pause. It is stopping to smell the roses in life as often as possible. It is a pause in all the mental "doing." Mindfulness meditation and mindfulness living is purposeful use of vibration to open the gate from thinking mind to that of *receptive mind*—from thought related to the past and the future to the nonthought of the present and of nowness. There are examples of meditations at the end of this chapter to get you started, and there are hundreds of excellent books on the art of mindful meditation.

Emotive Tools for Change

The third group of bridging tools comes from a place that is emotion centered. This group of bridging tools includes the emotion-based aspects known as *Gratitude, Forgiveness, Compassion, and Love*. Each has its own set of vibrations, and each is interwoven with the other. Here is a closer look at each:

Gratitude

Feeling gratitude is a logically pinpointing state of being. Probably one of its basic strengths for our use in gaining inner satisfaction comes from one simple fact: We cannot be angry, frustrated, sad, confused, or otherwise negative *at the same time* we are feeling grateful. They are mutually exclusive. Imagine feeling full of thankfulness while being angry: It's not possible. The ego is shut down when we experience gratitude. For this reason, allowing and promoting feelings of gratitude is one of the most effective tools in the addiction recovery field. Furthermore, it can create positive energy almost instantly for anyone.

There have been times when negative moods and states of mind have left me unable to think of anything for which I *felt* grateful. It is as if I am stuck in a negative place of muck and the thought of feeling even an ounce of thankfulness is unthinkable. A friend of mind once suggested that I come up with a gratitude list while in a positive frame of mine. I did so and saved it. It was pretty long and included the obvious things, such as health, friends, family, and personal possessions. Later on, I added less obvious things for which I was grateful. These included being possessed with the ability to make changes in my life; the ability to accept that which I cannot change; the ability to change my perception in order to let something be what it is—all the while knowing that it will likely change on its own someday. On days when I am not able to get into a grateful place, I pull that gratitude list out. I remind myself of what I have forgotten. Reading it with an open mind allows adjustment in my perception, which leads to a boost in how I feel.

True gratitude is well beyond words and thoughts of thanksgiving. Adding emotional energy to it is essential for gratitude to be true and authentic. This is why gratitude is in the emotional bridge category. Being open to that is all that is necessary. This is an emotion-based *letting go* effort.

Forgiveness

Forgiveness has been the topic of so many sermons, lectures, workshops, and books that virtually no one could deny the significance of the act of forgiveness. That being said, forgiveness has a significant caveat; it is not necessary—*if* you love unconditionally. Unconditional love, as we will see later, is not easily accomplished, so intentional forgiveness turns out to be necessary fairly often in life on a lower level of living. Deliberate acts of forgiveness begin with the *intention to* forgive; they do not usually begin with sincere *feelings* of forgiveness. That is the end result. Feeling forgiveness takes place because we have found a way to love unconditionally.

Another point about this type of reconciliation has to do with a little-known secret related to what, in fact, we are forgiving. Failing to forgive ourselves for our own transgressions is that little-known barrier to real absolution. Gary R. Renard, in his book, *The Disappearance of the Universe*, expands this idea of self-forgiveness in a very compelling read. Through Divine sources, Renard helps the reader see that neglecting to forgive ourselves creates an unhealed and destructive way of living. This agonizing perception acts as a trigger button for us at times when other people do similar or related acts; or simply reminds us of our own unfinished, unhealed past. The unwelcome reminder charges us with unhealed energy that we think is caused by the other person. In actuality, it is all about *our* lack of healing and *our* lack of self-forgiveness.

The bottom line is that the path to forgiving others is to forgive ourselves. This is really about allowing yourself to unconditionally love yourself. Loving your neighbor as yourself is a good goal. A higher intention is to love yourself unconditionally so that you can love your neighbor similarly. One of my mentors in life once said in a speech that failing to forgive is like taking poison and expecting the other person to die. That is not rational. Considering that real forgiveness begins with self-forgiveness makes the poison even more suicidal. There is no sweetness in that. We can do better.

Compassion

Compassion is perhaps the most emotion-bound of the transformation tools. Sometimes compassion seems very black and white, as if someone has it or not. Other times it appears that compassion is more an ideal than a heartfelt condition. In reality, compassion is about feelings of *empathy that express in the outer world.*

As a tool for bridging the Inner Self with the outer world, compassion is about allowing natural feelings of caring and kindness to express in both directions—Inner Self to others, other people to our Inner Selves. It is allowing vulnerability to be acceptable. It almost goes without saying that compassion only operates when forgiveness is taking place or love is already in place.

Love

Another topic with massive exposure to scrutiny is love. Compounding the issue of love is the fact that people in almost all cultures have come up with a multitude of types and categories of love. Agape love from the Bible, which is selfless, sacrificial, unconditional love; brotherly love; romantic love; love for mankind; love of things versus people; love of child; spiritual love; religious love; love in theory; and safe love are just a few of the categories of love that confuse us. These ideas alter our understanding of what *one* love is. This ego-driven process of taking something that is one and splitting it into many defined smaller aspects is fear-driven.

They are often sentimental and make for gut-wrenching lyrics for thousands of songs.

From God's point of view there is only *one love*. It is one vibrational element. It has varying rates so that less and less love does not change that it is love. It means that people may call the lower levels of love the terms fear or hate, but in the realm of vibration we are just experiencing less intensity of that *one* love. At the highest vibrational end is unconditional love.

Less love means that we are putting artificial conditions on our unconditional love. Hence, we are failing to experience unconditional love due to out-there conditions that we have arbitrarily applied to love. Likewise, we experience fear-based conditions because we are told to accept those out-there conditions. People in our family, society, and culture steer us wrong. We learn to fear. In God's view, there is love and it is unconditional. For humans that is a goal worth experiencing. That is a real tool for comfort.

Bridging out-there conditional love with inner unconditional love simply means we find a way to love no matter what. The idea is simple, but the accomplishing of it is often difficult. We can set our intentions to live life with more and more understanding and acceptance of unconditional love. We will, while in that type of energy, experience more and more unconditional love. It is assured.

Being Tools for Change

"Being" could be described as the ongoing manifestations of God qualities. It is a bridging that is about things we can practice in our daily lives that are "doing" things with a twist. These doing things are not for the sake of doing them, or for the rewards that may come about. Instead, they are about *doing* as a result of *being*.

The key tools include the aforementioned *love* along with the tools of *kindness, open-mindedness,* and *authenticity.* All four of these tools are initiated by setting an *intention*, having the *will* to move on it, and, finally, to *embody* it. To embody it is the *being* aspect.

Being Love

Being love is coming from a place of self-love. Loving your neighbor and those who we perceive as enemies is about removing anything that prevents you from loving yourself. Once that is achieved, which is accomplished by changing perceptions, you have the ability to embrace a certain unconditional self-love.

Being love is about coming from a place of love all the time, in all conditions, for all things and people. This, in turn, allows you to move and embody love in such a manner that you are essentially *being* love. To be sure, there will be times when the *being* gets challenging and may even seem absent for a minute, but *being love* is the ideal default condition—the cushy place to be.

Being Kindness

Being kind is different from *being kindness*. Just as with *being love*, *being kindness* is an embodiment of your every waking hour, your every effort in all interactions with others. It is beyond just doing kind things; it is being a person whose every intention is to be kind to all people under all conditions, even when cut off in traffic. There can be no room for sexism, ageism, racism, homophobia, antisemitism, xenophobia, Islamophobia, indifference, and the other fear-based mental positions. To *be* kindness, one's intention must be to have the habit of doing kindness from a heart that is always open, always free, and always loving.

Being Open-minded

Being open-minded is about having openness to things that are not already a part of our thinking, beliefs, and ways of being. It allows for evolution from primitive to sophisticated, from seed to fruition, from new to mature, and from ignorance to wisdom. Of all the bridges, *being* open-minded is the most fundamental since it allows and even encourages change, growth, and fresh awareness. Within any new awareness is the opportunity for moving from the notion that we can find true comfort out-there to the *knowing* that it is found inside our very *being*.

Being Authentic

Authenticity is about *being yourself*. It is about being honest in a fearless way at the level of *being*. This is so even if it reveals supposedly unpopular, unacceptable, uncouth, or self-deprecating qualities. There is the awareness of who and what we really are (that Inner Self part of you). Being authentic is about being humble, teachable, flexible, and respectful. Authenticity results from a willingness to stand naked in mind, body, and soul. It comes about from having the guts to have the intention, willingness, decisiveness, and effort to simply *be* what you are in any given moment. Discovering who and what you are is one of the main points of this book and is critical. Being authentic is the bravest thing you will ever do and it results from the culmination of all the other "being" aspects. Authenticity is about living in peace, joy, and love. Later, authenticity is studied in great depth as we discover unexpected aspects from the Principle of Gender.

FINDING TRUE INNER COMFORT

Neal's Story

The story of Neal illustrates how vibration and proper use of it can transform and transmute a person's life. Neal described his life as having a mild to high grade of depression—every waking hour. He believed that unexpected good in his life was not his to keep and that he was unacceptable on the inside.

A friend from his church invited Neal to join him at a well-known self-improvement seminar. During the weeklong workshops, Neal's beliefs were challenged minute by minute. He experienced significant confusion and pain for much of the time. To his credit, he did not give up.

Neal started having shifts in his awareness. He realized that whatever he focused on created more of the energy upon which he focused. Neal wanted to stop being a victim of his own beliefs. He learned to transform old negative beliefs about his sexuality. From the seminar activities he found liberation from tension, stress, distress, and blocks of thinking and creativity. A fellow participant, who was a long-term member of twelve-step meetings, helped Neal do what he called "Let go and let God" as he embraced compassion, forgiveness, gratitude, and love.

His new energy led Neal to a book that explained the art of mindful meditation. He started practicing the tips from the book and even though he did not know it he transmuted his very energy. Over time, the activities of his life evolved in small but significant ways. Encouraging his inner natural and innate joy, peace, and love, Neal learned that the opposite of depression is, in fact, expression. In the end, Neal felt an uncommon freedom and enjoyed a new sense of being authentic, of being himself. It was an amazing liberation far more than that of only his sexual orientation.

Review Points

- Knowing that the differences between the manifestations of Matter, Mind, and Spirit are the result of different rates of vibration arms us with tools to transform dis-eased aspects of life into those that put us at ease.
- The higher vibration rates a person operates upon, the higher the rate and more pleasant the vibration he or she will experience; we have a choice in how it is altered.
- Blockages in life are the result of unsound, limiting, or irrational beliefs and other lower-vibration-rate beliefs that we can transform in a deliberate and purposeful manner.
- We will not progress to a new vibration or allow the flow of energy if we are still holding on to that cherished old vibration; we must consciously let go of the paralyzing thoughts and feelings upon which we are already clinging.
- "Letting God" is about being in alignment with the easier flowing, nonconflicted energies found naturally all through the universe; it is avoiding always having it your own way.
- Innate Bridging Tools happen automatically and only require us to pay attention to and respond to our Divine gut feelings—intuition and instinct.
- Mental Bridging Tools open the door to true inner comfort. They are thoughts, prayer, visualization, affirmations, Masterminding, positive thinking, mindfulness, and meditation.
- The Emotive Bridging Tools allow us to tap into our own innate inner qualities. They are gratitude, forgiveness, compassion, and love.

- Being Bridging Tools are kindness, open-mindedness, love, and authenticity, which are initiated by setting an intention, having the will to move on it, and embodying it.
- Focusing only on what we desire purposely directs our very vibration to manifest our goals.

Affirmations

These Affirmations are based on what we have learned from *The Kybalion*. They are intended to be stand-alone statements to be used at times we notice that we have become stuck in some way.

> I accept change as fundamental to life.
>
> I know that changing perception changes life.
>
> I know that "this too shall pass"—including what I like and what I like less.
>
> I seek the desired vibration.
>
> I know that good is already in me.
>
> I take responsibility consciously in life.
>
> I do my best in thought and action.
>
> I manifest by focusing my attention only on what I desire.
>
> I let go of the lower-rate vibrations so they can move.
>
> I let God by letting the highest vibrations be my intentions.
>
> I practice living mindfully so the vibration of God is my "being."

Mindful Meditation Examples

Before getting into the examples, here are a few points and reminders about mindful meditation. The purpose of mindful meditation is to get into the spaces between your active thoughts, into the spaces of your mind where there is less thinking about the past or the future. The goal, then, is to be in the now moment; being aware of only what is present in this moment. It is a rest from the energies of worrying, regrets, planning, and other active or aimless thinking.

The best way to achieve this form of energy is to focus on something that is currently happening or is present in the environment. It could be the sound of a ticking clock, or the humming of an air-conditioning unit, or the tapping of someone's footsteps. It could be something visual, such as the flicker of a candle flame. For many, the use of mantras creates a steady focus. Perhaps most effective for most people is to focus on counting; the counting of breaths in and out.

It is best to mindfully meditate daily for at least five minutes, but twenty minutes twice a day is considered ideal. Mindful meditation builds on each experience in the same way working out with weights does for strength training: You can build strength and muscles only if you exercise regularly. To build your meditation muscles you will ideally meditate at least once a day; and twice a day is even better.

Without a doubt, random thoughts will enter your mind as you practice being mindful. When the aimless thoughts pop into your mind, gently remind yourself that your intention is to meditate and return to your counting, listening, images, and such. Be kind with yourself when the intruding thoughts come into your mind; and over time, as you practice over the weeks, you will notice that the intruding thoughts will happen less often.

Example 1—Counting/Images Mindful Meditation

a.) For at least five minutes, sit with eyes closed. Posture should be such that the crown of your head is pulled up and your back is straight. You can sit on a chair or cross-legged on the floor or ground, whichever is most comfortable for you.

b.) With eyes closed, begin counting your inhaled breaths and/or your exhaled breaths to the count of twelve. Repeat.

c.) Keeping your breathing normal and regular, imagine the numbers on a clock as you say them in your mind. After you reach the number twelve, see the 1 on the imagined clock and count "one;" repeat the counting over and over one through twelve along with your breaths and the images of the digits of the clock in your mind.

Example 2—Images Mindful Meditation

Follow **Example 1a**. Choose images that have positive energies for you, such as a seaside, woodlands, or sky.

Another form of Images Mindful Meditation is to actually use your eyes to see the images of something present, such as a candle flame. Use **Example 1a**. With this form of meditation, you have your eyes open as you focus on the object. A candle flame is ideal because it has movement and yet is comforting in its very being. You can add **Example 1b** to this form of meditation if that helps you keep your focus on the now moment.

Example 3—Listening Mindful Meditation

Follow **Example 1a**. *Place yourself somewhere that has repeated or predictable sounds, such as a ticking clock. Focus on the repeating sound. If other sounds occur, let them be in the background as you keep your focus only on the original recurring ticking.*

A variation of Listening Meditation *would be to add* **Example 1a, b, and c** *to the listening.*

Example 4—Walking Mindful Meditation

Mindfulness can take place with your eyes open and your body moving. Walking in nature, in a labyrinth, on a beach, or in a park with a "return to start" looping pathway is ideal for Walking Mindfulness. *This form of meditation takes a little more discipline but is deeply rewarding. The focus is more easily lost, since your eyes are open and can lead to a type of distraction that opens the door to random thoughts of the past and future. The objective with* Walking Mindful Meditation *is to keep your mind on the objects of nature, enjoying the sight of them as each one comes into view. It is to see the objects one at a time, not allowing your eyes' focus to move on to the next object until you have fully appreciated the current object. This is akin to the notion of stopping to smell the roses. Once you have fully appreciated the object, move on to the next.*

A variation of this meditation is to mindfully take in an entire scene. This could be focusing on the sky while you lay on your back in a lawn or field. You are focused on the movement of the clouds. Or it could be focusing on the sea horizon while you sit at the beach; any inspiring landscape will do. In these open-eyed meditations you are disciplining your mind to only see and entertain what you see; gently returning to that sight and refocus anytime thoughts of the past or future enter your mind. As with all meditation, it is a practice, not a perfection.

CHAPTER SIX
Being This and That

The **Principle of Polarity** explains that everything has two poles, and everything has its opposite. It allows us to understand that polarity is the Truth of the things that are of our Higher Power. This is in contrast to duality which is the common human understanding of what is real. Their differences are highly significant when we consider our intentions in life for removing our discomforts. The Principle of Polarity puts it this way:

> "Everything is dual; everything has poles; everything has its pairs of opposites; like and unlike are the same. Opposites are identical in nature, but different in degree; extremes meet; all truths are but half-truths; all paradoxes may be reconciled."
>
> —THE KYBALION

Although it may seem contradictory, it is a thought-provoking message wherein many perplexing and unexplained aspects of life are explainable with a deeper understanding of these accepted ideas. By accepting certain Divine Truths that seem to be opposing to our common understanding, we are on our way to finding true inner comfort. We also find other avenues for transforming, transcending, and transmuting the uncomfortable out-there aspects of life.

A Quick Breakdown of This and That

The statements "Everything is dual; everything has poles; everything has its pairs of opposites" do seem paradoxical, but in actuality it just means that everything can be perceived as this *or* that; as well as this *and* that with degrees in between.

Duality and polarity are not exclusive ideas, but polarity certainly allows a better understanding of how to derive true lasting pleasure in life.

The statements "Like and unlike are the same. Opposites are identical in nature, but different in degree" zero in on the idea that even though entities exist somewhere with an opposite, they are, in reality, degrees of the same thing along a continuum (pole). So, there are, indeed, extremes, but most things exist somewhere in between those extremes.

The duality concept is a human understanding of the material world of reality; polarity is a higher or spiritual understanding from God's perspective—Truth, if you will.

That "extremes meet" statement explains how life and all things of the Universe are eternal. The extremes, seen far enough along the continuum, never actually end and therefore connect again. One way to envision this is in the form of a ring, which is technically a pole that circles back to its beginning. Another image is the infinity symbol that is shaped like figure eight. Such principles are very thought-provoking and have stirred endless conversations among scholars, philosophers, scientists, and religious academics for centuries. It is a concept of eternity that is presented in *The Kybalion* as another aspect of The All; no real beginning or ending.

The statements that "all truths are but half-truths; all paradoxes may be reconciled" point to the fact that there is always more to know: more aspects to consider when looking at life and the existence of all things. This point has much to do with explaining the unexplained—we just don't have all the facts within our understanding, nor can we. The desire to understand all the mysteries of life is reasonable, but our failure to understand everything is predictable. Closer to home, the desire to discover why our partner in life does what he or she does also lets us know we cannot know everything about any person, including ourselves.

Duality Versus Polarity

While all the Principle of Polarity ideas are helpful in our effort to find lasting enjoyment, the duality and polarity aspects are two of the most important. Consider that duality thinking creates most of the discomfort in life; and polarity is the true nature of all things. Furthermore, polarity offers several key tools for purposeful change. These polarity tools are additional paths to transformation, transmutation, and transcendence.

In the human experience, we have duality. We see things as yes or no, black or white, light or dark, good or bad, high or low,

Heavenly Father or hellish demon, perfect or wrong, ripe or spoiled. The list goes on with such conditions as rich or poor, love or hate, peace or conflict, and rejection or acceptance—all leading the way to painful ways of living.

The ancient "yin yang" symbol illustrates the dualism aspects in an artful manner of Chinese origins. Black and white, it shows how opposite energies can be both dueling and complementary in natural life. It lacks the grays of polarity.

A redesigned "yin yang" symbol illustration shows how polarity can be viewed with energies that include all aspects—the black, white, and grays. A life of true inner comfort embraces all degrees.

We tend to think and make decisions based on those extremes even though when we rationally consider them we know that there are degrees of things in between:

- Good and evil and something that is not quite evil but not quite good according to our dual-based judgment
- Black and white and shades of gray
- Up and down and maybe over to the side somewhere
- Hot and cold and some degree of warm or cool
- Rich and poor and degrees of middle class

Considering the Principle of Vibration, we know that all those aspects are really the same thing, within its type—just on a different vibration setting. With the Principle of Polarity, we take it a step further and see that each entity is on one pole. Hot and cold are on the same pole with their different vibrations being the thing that allows us to label them as hot or cold, along with some degree of warm in between. As a result, all manifested things have two apparent ends; two aspects that can run the extremes and everything in between. This is Polarity.

Polarity is inclusive, while duality looks at just two opposing aspects. We have the right to view things as black or white. The All, on the other hand, is inclusive in nature and would see it *as* all shades of the black, gray, and white spectrum. There is good because we evaluate it as so. There are also infinite degrees of pleasant and not so pleasing. For us, it is a matter of judgment. This makes polarity even more important to understand.

The understanding is that everything *is* and is *not* at the same time; and that all truths are but half-truths while every truth is half not true. We would have polarities of almost yes or almost no, less and more lightness, good and less good, various elevations of not hot and cold, and a multitude of other degrees of manifestations.

We acknowledge that there are two apparent sides to everything, yet things that appear as opposites are identical in nature. The polarity between perfect and imperfect could be seen as this: It is what it is *and* it is to our liking to various degrees.

This higher level of understanding emphasizes that what seems to be opposite to the other (duality) is actually the same—just with different degrees of its vibration. We could see fruit as ripe or spoiled in a dual perspective; or from a polarity perspective we would see the fruit as ripe and less ripe. To be more precise, from the polarity perspective the fruit goes in two directions of overly ripe on one end and some degree of not yet ripe at the other end.

Paradoxes Reconciled

If we think of a pole, we can see a straight line with two ends. It is not as easy to see that the extremes meet. Follow along on this example: East and west are extremes. Let's say we travel east in a jet and arrive to a place that was referred to as west (let's say Denver, which is west of my hometown of Toledo). When we arrive over Denver, it is no longer west (it is here). And if we continue on the western path and pass Denver, Denver is seen then as east.

Or consider this: If we jet along in a northerly direction far enough over the earth, we begin to head south on the other side of the earth. Our seemingly straight line, then, can actually be viewed more as a ring, the never-ending line that does, in this illustration, have different vibration rates depending on the point in question. When we sit at the seashore and look at the horizon, it appears to be a straight line. In fact, though, it has a curve that is not perceivable from our vantage point. This is one example of the reconciliation of paradoxes. It is a matter of perception.

We realize, with this polarity principle, that all paradoxes may be reconciled if we have all the information—but then there is no "all" information to have since it is infinite. It is another paradox.

The endless ring that represents the pole of vibration offers another example: This one has to do with Spirit and Matter being One. All is one. This can be reconciled by the seemingly straight pole being shaped like a ring. Matter (slower vibration) and Spirit (higher vibration) are two poles of the same thing. Polarity, by its very definition, is about Oneness. One thing has two extreme aspects. A pole has two poles or two ends, yet the ends must meet. Therefore, they are the same thing vibrating at different rates; another way of seeing Oneness.

Contrast this with duality. Duality describes two things: this *or* that; not this *and* that, as one. Duality exists in the human domain for the purpose of understanding and explaining. It takes judgment to do that. We believe in duality in our daily living, but to experience a greater degree of comfort we must engage the idea of polarity.

The downside of duality is that we become tired, unhappy, and off-balance because of cross, or dueling, thoughts. Conflicted thoughts are tiring, frustrating, and maddening.

Still, in the real world we tend to want to label things according to our likes and dislikes, our comfort and discomfort, and take the extremes to prove our point. We label things that way. This not only does not satisfy any comfort-seeking, it actually creates more discomfort.

A Short Trip to Eden

In theory and tradition, there was a time free of duality for mankind. The story that nicely illustrates this is one of the oldest and most well-known of all—the story of Adam, Eve, and the Serpent in a place East of what was known as Eden. I use this story not because one must believe that it actually took place, but because it is a good account for illustrating the comfort-seeking nature of mankind. I like it, too, because of its broad familiarity to Jewish, Christian, and Muslim cultures.

In the beginning God created everything. The Bible makes it clear that God viewed everything as good at the end of each day. Every step of the way, it is declared good, including the Adam and Eve creations.

Adam and Eve lived in the perfect place with no strife and in total harmony. All was good. Since all was good there was no bad. Or at least nothing was judged because what was to judge? Adam and Eve had the bliss of living in the now moment and simply just "being" with God and all God's creations. Adam and Eve were free to enjoy all aspects of the Garden of Eden because they had freedom of choice.

However, as we know, there was a rule in Eden. Adam and Eve were not to eat the fruit from the Tree of the Knowledge of Good and Evil. Of all things, it was that type of fruit. As it is told, if they ate from this certain tree they would die. Implied in this story is that Adam and Eve did *not* have knowledge about the distinctions between the labels of good and evil. The duality of good and evil apparently existed, but only God had that knowledge—at least until Eve and then Adam did eat the fruit from the Tree of the Knowledge of Good and Evil. They, indeed, did choose to have the knowledge of good and evil. In a shortsighted way, they chose to see Eden in duality.

Due to that freedom of choice, Adam and Eve had the ability to judge for themselves about all things of Eden. In an instant, the bounty, beauty, and harmony of Eden was forever changed—in perception. Eden no longer appeared so perfectly wonderful because Adam and Eve began judging the good versus the bad.

Without the knowledge of good and evil, Adam and Eve only knew "it is what it is." My interpretation is that in their judgment of good versus evil Adam and Eve automatically died as "beings." They were not punished by a death of their bodies; they simply experienced the outcome of judgment. They were no longer enjoying everything as varying degrees of good. Instead they perceived things, judged things, and created a land of duality, conflict, confusion, pain, and lack. This was a death, of sorts.

In that same instant of the awareness of duality there became a seemingly necessary protector. The newly perceived negativity produced the concept of *ego* in Adam and Eve; and ego appeared in all the generations that followed. This was a pretty uncomfortable new development. Their newly formed protective device—ego—was very helpful in giving *temporary* comfort.

The Eden story gives an example of the creation of ego. Adam and Eve apparently always enjoyed their naked bodies. Their bodies were considered good. After eating the fruit of the forbidden tree, they saw their differences as female and male. In their confusion about those differences, their awareness shifted from "all is good in the land of Eden" to dual-based judgment. Their egos took charge. Suddenly Adam is saying something like "Eve, our body differences are not as good as we thought and we shall call those differences bad and shameful. And, oh, I think we should cover ourselves before God notices our differences. Grab some fig leaves, honey!"

Eden did not change: Adam and Eve changed from having an accepting point of view of their lives. They were no longer simply "being" in Eden. They were "doing" Eden. They were living from the outside inward—the same ego-driven lives as we have today. Make no mistake: Dis-ease all starts with dual-based judgment calls.

- Eden—a place of ongoing comfort because "being" was the condition of life. Being in alignment with God (Thy will be done) was the way of life.
- Leaving Eden—a place of ongoing discomfort because "doing" resulted from all the dual-viewed perceptions and judgment wherein the ego drives the need to have it "our way."

From this understanding we have the awareness that there are infinite possibilities and that viewing things as either this *or* that limits our experience and frustrates our life. In life, "It is what it is." Judgment is a human device that creates division, separateness, and uncomfortable feelings that are not necessary and are not part of any lasting comfort.

It is important to remember that any given unpleasant aspect of life is simply a point. It is not good or bad except by perception. If we find that we are uncomfortable with something, we can know that it will be changing as the result of causes and effects. We know that we can change things by changing our perception. In this way, the good thing that is not of our liking can be better. And better. And still better. It would eventually reach a place that was good enough to be comfortable.

We have the freedom to choose to abstain from judgement. When you come down to it, most things don't really warrant the effort it takes to judge them and then emotionally react to them.

Freedom of Choice in Direction

This leads to the even better news. We can find more comfort from perceiving life's endless details as part of lower and higher vibration rates on the same standard or pole. This has to do with the nature of the poles. The Principle of Polarity tells us that two poles can be classified as Positive and Negative in the same way as the Earth's magnetic poles. It states:

> "Love is positive to hate. Courage to fear. Activity to Non-Activity."
>
> —**THE KYBALION**

There is an exciting tendency of Nature: These negative and positive poles tend to move in the direction of the dominant activity, which is toward the positive pole. Things naturally tend to move in the positive course because we keep looking in that positive direction; longing for those encouraging things as a whole. The higher vibration is just more enjoyable—remember that at the highest rate of vibration, The All vibration rate is so high that it is almost at rest. At rest is soothing, indeed.

The more desirable things in life tend to dominate the lesser dominant things, which are the negative things. We have the freedom of choice to look the other way and focus negatively, but that is not our natural tendency. For example, we tend toward love rather than lesser love. We favor peace rather than less peace. We move toward prosperity rather than less prosperity. This process happens automatically.

All things of the Universe, including us, have a natural movement toward positive. It is an encouraging flow that is easier to maneuver than rowing against the current.

Conversely, we also sometimes focus our attention on our fears and discomforts. Most likely it is in an unconscious manner. We can focus on fear and bring in so much fear that our lives become consumed by it. This fear thing is the basis for our egos. Ego, as I am using the term, is simply a fear-based point of view that uses temporary out-there comforters to offset our discomfort. Perhaps this is akin to our concept of original sin, which is a reference to that forbidden fruit incident in the Garden of Eden. Our freedom of choice seems automatic and operates on an unconscious level, and when fear is present it is a negative direction. The blessing is that negative is not the default track.

Consciously Living within the Continuum

In explaining a key aspect of the Principle of Polarity, *The Kybalion* authors state this: **"Things belonging to different classes cannot be transmuted into each other, but things of the same class may be changed, they may have their polarity changed. Thus, love never becomes East or West, or Red or Violet—but it may and often does turn into Hate."**

We are aware that with our own willingness and perception we can change the direction of consciousness by changing our focus. This statement emphasizes that it *must* be *within the continuum* of our intention. How does that work? That is the most exciting part of the Principle of Polarity, perhaps the most powerful thing of all the ideas put forth in *The Kybalion*. It is done by literally *willing* and *visualizing* a higher vibration on the pole of the issue at hand. Energy workers and healers know of what I am referring. For example, we can take the duality term of poverty at the lower vibration end and *will* it to higher prosperity on the same continuum.

In contrast, the reality is that most people are usually looking for things in all the wrong places. Let's look at some common examples wherein we are looking for solutions of dis-ease by jumping from one pole to another.

Take the example of the man who wants to feel better about himself so he sets his sights on being rich. He does everything in his power to make lots of money. This satisfies his ego, but he never has enough money and still does not feel better about himself. Why? He is working on different poles in the land of polarity. His feelings of self-worth are on the polarity pole related to his being. Being a good person and having integrity and authenticity would truly satisfy.

Instead, however, this man's efforts are on a different polarity pole altogether—all related to money. Self-worth and money are not on the same continuum of vibration.

Another example is the child who wants to feel loved and somehow learns to accept getting attention instead—attention of any sort, good and bad. This unhappy child exhibits all sorts of unappreciated behavior and attitudes that displease people but give him attention. *Love* and *attention* are not on the same continuum nor in the same class.

There is the teenage girl who feels bad about her appearance. So, she eats comfort foods. Eating is not on the same continuum as self-esteem and she gains unwanted weight. As she looks at herself she judges herself negatively. The food choice worsens the outlook.

What of the man who feels torment about having been sexually molested as a boy and uses pornography endlessly to "feel good"? He needs forgiveness but goes after sexual stimulation instead. His pain is only dulled by the pornography; it is not overcome. He ends up feeling shame, not forgiveness. Sexual satisfaction is on a different continuum from forgiveness.

Looking for solace in all the wrong places is about looking out-there and looking in a mistaken continuum. This is the primary reason looking out-there does not work. Out-there is usually on a different continuum—not always, but most often.

Jackson's Story

The real-life story of Jackson is an example of the value of polarity being discovered after the discomfort of duality thinking had taken over his life.

Jackson was a highly effective manager who knew how to get things done. His small but productive department at work had always had its ups and downs, but nothing that could not easily be handled. Jackson always came up with a plan to correct things.

There came a time, however, when things took a nose-dive. Over a two-month period, Jackson's department lost one full-time employee to a serious illness that resulted in early and unexpected retirement; and then the only other full-time employee resigned. With these two events, Jackson was the only full-time employee left. He started complaining as he felt the lower vibrations of lack. From the polarity standpoint, we could say he was focused on the lower part of the Abundance Pole.

The out-there dualities Jackson came up with were seemingly great remedies. They fell short. Resentment set in. Jackson reached a point where he wanted to quit his job. And yet his ego told him that he could not live with himself if he left under such dire conditions. He was actually going further down in the vibration of the Abundance Pole. He was not aware of that pole and was only aware of "I am not getting relief and it is bad." Duality. Sinking further down the Abundance Pole, Jackson saw no abundance at all. He only saw lack.

The spiritual director of his church happened to call him about another matter just when things could not get worse. Seizing the opportunity, Jackson started unloading and venting like a crazy man. The spiritual leader listened silently; and then told him a story that helped Jackson return to his own power. It is a classic Zen story that Jackson had heard years before, but never fully understood.

Is That So?

The ancient story goes something like this: A girl in a small village got pregnant. Her angry parents demanded to know who the father

BEING THIS AND THAT

was. At first resistant to answer, the anxious girl finally pointed to a well-known Zen master who had always been revered for living a pure life. When the outraged parents confronted this Zen master with their daughter's accusation, he simply replied, "Is that so?"

When the child was born, the parents brought it to the Zen master, who now was viewed as a pariah by the whole village. The parents demanded that he take care of the child since it was his responsibility. He said, "Is that so?" and calmly accepted the child.

For many months he took very good care of the child, until the daughter could no longer live with the lie she had told. She confessed that the real father was a young man in the village whom she had tried to protect.

The parents immediately went to the Zen master to reunite the baby with its mother. With profuse apologies they explained what had happened. "Is that so?" the Zen master said as he handed over the child.

The moral of the story...

The Zen Master could have gone into a panic by stating that the story was a lie and he was innocent. He could have, as did Jackson, looked at the facts and become overwhelmed. Instead he stayed calm, with the knowledge that he did not need to accept the perception of a problem. No, the Zen master chose to perceive the situation from an inner place—a place of Truth, not out-there facts. The Truth was a place of polarity instead of duality. The issue was that the frightened girl presented facts that were not true. The Zen master found comfort in knowing the Truth and staying with that polarity aspect.

This contrasted with Jackson, who let the out-there facts of his job jump-start his ego into thinking that he would find peace in other out-there solutions. He, as did the Zen master, could have found peace by seeking it from within himself—where peace exists for everyone. Duality of the out-there ego trapped Jackson into thinking the solutions are out-there. Polarity is about looking within, knowing that an abundance of peace (the solution to his overwhelm) was about focusing on peace and the energy of more and more peace—staying on that pole.

With a reminding from his spiritual director, Jackson saw that he could change the negative direction of consciousness by changing focus within the continuum of intention—which was to be in alignment with the energies of God—not to see a human's own plan be fulfilled. Although he was not aware of it, Jackson's ego had convinced him that the solutions could only be found in the place of duality.

In the end, Jackson stopped making decisions based on his ego's fear of guilt in leaving his position under those dire straits. He had been offered a position with another company, and with his new freedom of "being" he accepted it with no regrets. He was focused on the Abundance Pole and clearly saw that what he wanted and needed could be found in letting go of fear.

Visualize Getting Jacked Up

From these ideas we can conclude that in order to raise the conditions of our life we have to address the issue within the same continuum. Addressing the issue is about raising the vibration on the polarity pole—not jumping to another pole. Consider this: I will focus on the abundance and on raising my awareness. I will raise my awareness of prosperity on all levels—health, talent, finances, relationships, and such. To be effective, I must stay on the continuum of prosperity and raise the vibration. How does that work?

Several years ago, I bought my house knowing that it had some old-house settling issues. I hired a guy to literally jack up the house in the sagging places just as you would jack up a car to change its tire. The difference was, of course, it was a house; a huge and heavy house! It never occurred to me that someone could jack up something so heavy. The contractor very slowly raised up the house foundation over the course of weeks. Focusing and using as many of the Bridging Tools as are needed to get the job done is how to jack up life—which may or may not be heavy. It is how we can imagine moving the vibration level on the pole.

Final Thoughts on Polarity

With the knowledge of the Principle of Polarity, we know that we can stop judging things in life and take action that truly deals with the real solutions—or at least creates the satisfying comfort. So instead of saying, "I am unhappy so I need love," we can visualize a lifting of the unhappy to increased happy. Love will probably come along anyway, but not because we go looking for it (a doing thing). In this way we avoid the land mine of duality actions in favor of the force and power of God; using the very nature of creation to increase what we want by moving away from what is uncomfortable toward what is more comfortable. These qualities, as depicted in the Sun center of the Life Source illustration, are internally there for us, if we choose to seek comfort there.

It behooves us to remember that Adam and Eve started out in the energies of "being." Being love, peace, bliss, and harmony were Eden things. They did not need any strategies for dealing with negatives because they perceived none. After knowledge of good and evil became their way of perception, their egos took over and all hell broke loose. We do not have to live in those ego-driven ways when we consider the Principle of Polarity.

It seems appropriate to conclude this chapter with a direct quote from *The Kybalion* authors. It is from the last paragraph of the chapter on the Principle of Polarity. It says it all. **"A knowledge of the existence of this great Hermetic Principle will enable the student to better understand his own mental states, and those of other people. He will see that these states are all matters of degree, and seeing thus, he will be able to raise or lower the vibration at will—to change his mental poles, and thus be Master of his mental states, instead of being their servant and slave."**

Review Points

- Knowing the differences between Duality and Polarity is significant when we consider our intentions in life for easing our discomforts.
- Duality is an either/or human understanding of the material world of reality.
- Polarity is an inclusive higher or spiritual understanding from God's perspective.
- There are infinite possibilities. Viewing things as either this or that limits our experience and *frustrates* our life; it is liberating to see all of life as this *and* that.

- Looking for comfort in all the wrong places is about looking out-there and looking in the wrong polarity continuum; we will not find love if we are looking for it on the continuum of money.
- We can choose comfort in being free of judgment and knowing "it is what it is."
- By using visualization of a higher vibration of the same class (the same polarity continuum) we can change any life experience.

Guided Meditation

Probably the best way to use this guided meditation or any guided meditation is by listening to it as you follow its directions. Feel free to record this one and make it your own with changes as feels right. Over time, you may make up your own transformational story and ad lib it as you go. It is still a guided meditation.

Sit comfortably with eyes closed.
Picture yourself sitting in whatever environment that you are actually in.
As you sit, review in your mind a situation, feeling, or way of being that somehow seems unacceptable to you. See this outer-world aspect of your life in all of its parts. Now, set an intention to change the energy of that outer-world aspect to a higher rate of vibration. Know that you have the ability to do this with your own mental processes. In your mind's eye, recall your most favorite, safe, and relaxing place. Picture it in all its details, sights, sounds, and smells.

See yourself moving out of your sitting position and taking whatever mode of transportation that you wish, or the one that makes the most sense—by foot, by car, by plane, by hot air balloon, by teleport, by etherical eminence—then choosing one; and see yourself enjoying the journey. Take as long as you wish—a few seconds or, if you dare, a few hours. Find yourself arriving to your destination safe and sound; and in a creative and receptive state of mind.

As you arrive at your favorite place, notice beneath you, at your feet, a box. See that it is a most intriguing box and note that you have the urge to see inside it. Upon closer inspection of the outside of the box you see a label. On the label, see the very words of that aspect of your life that you want to change. See the words of that undesired aspect.

Imagine opening the box's lid and, as you do, watch a pole rise out of it high into the sky. It appears endless. Take a close look at the pole and notice that it is labeled, not necessarily with the issue you brought. It is labeled with the God quality you desire.

Recall with gratitude that the pole is the image that prevents you from jumping to a different, out-there solution—it keeps you on track.

Perhaps it is love, peace, joy, or abundance. Be mindful of the quality that applies to your desire, to the thing that will comfort you. On that pole, note that it is marked with an arrow that says, "You are here."

Know in your mind and heart that you have the ability to lift that arrow to a higher place on that pole. You can move the vibration rate with your mind, with the One Mind.

See the arrow move up the pole. Imagine how it feels to be experiencing life at that higher level. More love, more peace, more joy, more abundance—whichever applies to you. Imagine how it looks to be living life at this more comfortable level of being. See yourself being in that new place on the pole.

Continue to raise the vibrations, images, and sensations of that new level of polarity, and know that you can return to this place any time you choose. Languish in that place for as long as you like.

When you are ready, return to your original place while the arrow on the pole remains in its higher position; knowing that your efforts have had an impact on your life. You have raised the vibrations of life and found satisfaction with the inner qualities that have always been there. Know it, accept it, and be it.

CHAPTER SEVEN
Being Confident

Closely related to the Principle of Polarity is the **Principle of Rhythm**, which embodies the idea that everything manifested is in a measured motion, a to and fro, an outflow and inflow, a swing backward and forward, a pendulum-like movement. This principle explains that there is rhythm between every pair of opposites, or poles. The principle states:

> "Everything flows out and in; everything has its tides; all things rise and fall; the pendulum-swing manifests in everything; the measure of the swing to the right, is the measure of the swing to the left; rhythm compensates."
>
> —THE KYBALION

Three Planes of Rhythm

The Principle of Rhythm, as with all the principles, works with the notion of "As above, so below; as below, so above," which includes the various planes of physical, mental, and spiritual. A look at each is helpful in grasping the implications related to the flows of life as described in the Principle of Rhythm. Understanding the flows of life helps set limits that in turn helps us in finding true inner comfort.

Physical-plane Rhythm

In the physical plane of rhythm, we take the Principle of Polarity and show a certain predictability factor associated with motion. It is like the pendulum of a clock, the tides of the oceans, and the changes of the seasons. The cycles of life fall into the category of the rhythm of birth, life, death, and rebirth.

This idea solidifies the notion that change is inevitable, but in a reassuring manner, since change has some predictability. It states that it is predictable in its swing to the right and then left. Our reassurance level is related to this predictability. Night comes after day. After day comes night again. Death comes after life. After death comes a new life. The four seasons repeat year after year.

Mental-plane Rhythm

Physical plane aspects of the rhythm of life are obviously predictable even with the most casual observation. Less obvious are the many mental-plane aspects of life. Awake comes after sleep, and we return to sleep after a time of being awake. The unconscious is followed by the conscious, and in another life, it goes back to unconscious. The dark mood of regret is followed by the light mood of serenity.

This correspondence follows on the same continuum that we discovered in the Principle of Polarity: the season of summer is not followed by the color of purple. The feeling of love is not followed by the time of day known as night. Everything stays in its own continuum. Using the same image that we used in the Principle of Polarity, it stays on its own pole.

Spiritual-plane Rhythm

Certain conclusions about spiritual rhythms can be made that are significant to our quest for finding true inner comfort. Most significant and obvious is the fact that just as there are predicable physical ebbs and tides, there are predicable spirit-based movements.

Spiritual qualities have their own schedules, mysterious as they may be. Said another way, spiritually based characteristics such as love, peace, and joy have their own seasons. There will be times when we have unexplained and deep emotional shifts. For instance, love and peace are spiritual qualities that are ever-present within us. Even with that, however, they have their own spiritual movements. Although each is a constant unchanging quality within our very being, their limited movements often are out-pictured in the out-there life in more extreme ways. When we accept that these movements are natural, we can have a certain confidence that all is well despite appearances. This inevitable change of life is part of a natural and Divine process that is predictable and, therefore, not to be feared.

It is important to note that the ebbs and tides are our perceptions—not Truth-based. Peace, love, and joy do not of themselves alter to any degree. Our perceptions, as impacted by our fear-based ego, sound an alarm that is unjustified. Perception changes can be accepted as distorted (from fear). It is with reassuring awareness that the out-there movement of love, peace, and joy is not the Real inner love, peace, and joy. Furthermore, we know that the outer perceptions are part of something not understood in full.

Even if the sudden unexplained changes in our spiritual sensations are not always desirable or relieving, we can be comforted in knowing they will return to more pleasing places even if we do nothing. The greater Truth is that we still have inner love, peace, or joy no matter what perceptions we may have at any given time.

Perceived Lack of Control

For some, however, the greater Truth does not address a certain fly in the soup. We still tend to fight change of any kind. The Principle of Rhythm would seem to say that resistance to the inevitable evolution within the cycles of life is futile. We may feel comfortable with the idea that love is always on the continuum with less love. We may not like it when the pendulum swings into perceptions of less and less love to the point we call fear.

At first glance the Principle of Rhythm gives us the feeling that we have no control over the things that are happening around us as they naturally do their ebbing and flowing, expanding and shrinking, gaining and losing, in-breathing and out-breathing, and having and releasing. So, too, after shrinking, it expands; after losing, we gain; and after it releases, it returns to having. That is the positive direction that we tend to enjoy.

There is more to the story when we leave the physical plane and consider the mental realm. There is a certain type of grace found in the Hermetic understanding of the Principle of Rhythm. This is related to *predicting* and *managing* our mental ebb and flow movements.

At least one significant difference between the laws of polarity and the laws of rhythm exists. Both principles embrace the notion of continuum of polarity; however, the way in which we can manage our lives as related to polarities is different. From the Principle of Polarity, we learned that we can change conditions by *transforming* them by way of focusing on the energies of the polarities themselves. We focus on the higher vibration in order to find a more satisfying and comforting energy within that polarity.

It is possible to jump from the polarity of our Unconscious Mind to our Conscious Mind for the purpose of easing our dis-ease.

Our understanding of the Principle of Rhythm reveals that we change the mental conditions by *transmutation*. Rather than keeping to the same polarity, we can jump to another closely related one. This is not to say that we would jump from the love polarity to the financial polarity. It is a different type of jumping. In the mental plane exist two subplanes; the *Unconscious Mind* and the *Conscious Mind*. These two subplanes operate very closely with each other but have different levels of vibration that allow for our awareness of different perceptions.

Conscious Addressing of Negative Thoughts

The Planes of Consciousness are referred to as Lower and Higher. The Lower Plane is the *Unconscious Mind* while the Higher Plane is the *Conscious Mind*. It is important to recall that the Lower Plane is a slower rate of vibration than the Higher Plane.

Built within both the Lower and Higher Planes is what can be considered a parallel continuum. It exists with welcome polarity that enables us as humans to manage emotions and moods. This management tool is a *transmutation* process; we can take charge of our comfort levels mentally.

What saves us is our own awareness of the conscious and unconscious aspects of our minds. We must remember that they are two separate planes of mental operation but are closely related in nature. When the pleasing aspects of the unconscious naturally move into the less pleasing aspects, we can deliberately move our awareness energies from the unconscious to the conscious—presumably a more pleasing place. Allowing ourselves to passively wallow in the distressing aspects of an unconscious cycle is a set-up for a lifetime of depression, frustration, and anger. By taking charge of the situation, we can choose positive; we consciously have the choice to focus on positive ideas.

Some of the ways this can work:

- We can simply think and stay focused on positive ideas.
- We can focus on that for which we feel and are grateful.
- We can train ourselves to think of the positive aspects of life that may not be on the forefront but are nonetheless ever-present.
- We can also raise our awareness to the greater Truth of life.

We recognize that we can change anything in our experience if we *will it*. This movement from unconscious to conscious gives us some power or control that we feel we have lost because all things are part of a cycle and rhythm of life. As we have already seen, we have the choice to think on the positive side of things. What is new here is knowing that we have the choice to live consciously rather than unconsciously. Let's face it, living from an unconscious mind, that is to say *mindlessly*, is like living on some automatic, emotional roller coaster.

Awareness of the cycles as outlined in the Principle of Rhythm allows us to develop ways to manage uncomfortable emotional states of mind and do so in a conscious manner. We can learn about living consciously rather than unconsciously when the aspects of life that we don't like present themselves. Living consciously allows us to shift our own level of consciousness on a permanent basis.

Neutralization

Furthermore, *The Kybalion* claims that a person is able, to a great degree, to escape the swing toward pain by the process called Neutralization. This can take place even as the pain continues underfoot. By way of our awareness, we can avoid the *effects* of the pain. What are the implications if we get rid of the effects of pain? What is left?

At this point, it probably is helpful to remind ourselves that the uncomfortable effects that we do not avoid serve us nonetheless. This is true because the experience of positive effects is bound to occur by way of the natural flow toward positive from negative. It is our knowing that comfortable higher vibrations will follow the experience of less comfortable vibration. It is also useful to know that what you may consider unnerving may be unnoticeable to me and a pleasure to someone else. We all have our own perceptions.

> *There is comfort in knowing that pain and suffering are not the result of some "pay it forward" cycle, but instead the discomforts simply make way for a truer experience of what pleasure and joy are through the contrasts of their lack.*

The satisfying thing about this idea is a knowing that life tends to move from pain and suffering to joy and pleasure. When we combine this with the Law of Neutralization, wherein we can rise above pain and suffering with our thinking, we are aware that, truly, there is no reason to live a life of suffering. Even if the conditions are painful, our consciousness Mind can know pleasure, serenity, and comfort.

Transmutation of Unsound Beliefs

All that sounds great, but there are many times that thoughts alone are not the cause of suffering. When the cycle of our moods and states of mind still do not change, there is something more steadfast in place. This is directly related to our *core beliefs*. Core beliefs tend to run the show, so to speak, from behind the curtain. They are *out-there*. This is to say that core beliefs are usually not ideas of our conscious mind, yet they routinely impact our lives in predictable ways.

The Principle of Rhythm exposes yet another tool, an additional strategy to address that collection of thoughts that unite to form powerful beliefs. In simplest terms we mentally move from Unconscious Mind to Conscious Mind as related to whatever unsound, irrational, or limiting core beliefs we may have. Going from a life based on unhealthy unconscious beliefs to that of new healthy conscious beliefs is the goal here. A reminder: The Unconscious Mind is not good or bad; it just *is*.

Of utmost importance is the distinction that Unconscious Mind is on its own plane with its own polarity pole and Conscious Mind is on a higher plane with its own polarity pole. Both mental states run parallel to each other and work *with* each other for the advancement of each life. Operating from the Conscious Mind is natural and powerful. Operating from the Unconscious Mind is also natural as it allows a lot of helpful automatic responses in life.

Jumping from one polarity to another on purpose seems problematic and maybe even inadvisable when we think of the rules of Polarity. It is not impossible or inadvisable for the human mind when it is equipped with the right knowledge. The ebb of the unconscious mental state often enters the negative realm because of the effects of our beliefs. We do *not* have to remain there. We can purposely transmute our mind activities from the uncomfortable unconscious into the comfort of positive conscious beliefs. This is a form of alchemy. This transmuting allows us to experience conscious comfort by transforming from the cycle of painful unconscious vibrations.

Transmutation begins with *changing our perceptions*. This belief-changing strategy alters our old (usually) hidden irrational, unsound, and limiting unconscious beliefs. The best illustration of this transmutation is related to a behavioral health process known to psychologists for several decades.

Cognitive Behavioral Therapy

I first learned of the methods of Cognitive Behavioral Therapy as an undergrad student while studying to become a special education teacher. In hindsight, I see that the behavioral sciences caught up with the ancient Principle of Rhythm. Cognitive Behavioral Therapy was so impacting to my life that later it became the primary topic of my coursework in graduate school.

CBT, which is the common reference for Cognitive Behavioral Therapy, is a highly effective transmutation process of replacing fear-based beliefs in order to soothe uncomfortable feelings and resulting behavior.

What I learned was that a simple belief-creation process takes place in human life every time something new happens. In simplest form, it can be illustrated in the following formula:

- Something happens → we perceive → we give meaning → we respond (mentally, emotionally, and/or behaviorally)
- Happens again → repeat perception → meaning becomes belief → we react
- Happens repeatedly → perception fades → belief fades → we react automatically
- Something happens → we react

It turns out that one limiting aspect of this process is that our conclusions are often based on naive and fearful perceptions. This is so because most of the time those "Something happens" events take place initially during childhood. A child, of course, has naive and limited understandings of the world. These perceptions are always distorted by other childish half-truths and untruths. The hidden beliefs have become part of our unconscious processes as based on perceptions that are highly limited and distorted; and they nonetheless become core beliefs.

The process of Cognitive Behavioral Therapy uses the same model's series of events for the purpose of swapping out unwanted, unsound, limited, and irrational behaviors. Using transmutation strategies requires conscious use of the same steps and doing so with intention. We do this cognitively (by thinking) and it uses our *will* to change. As a result, the sequence of events for changing beliefs copies the very steps that created them. The original sequence:

- Something happens → we perceive → we give meaning → we respond

Using the same steps, CBT encourages transmutation in this way:

- Something happens → new conscious perception → new adult meaning → new deliberate response
- Happens again → repeat new perception → give meaning a rational belief → react
- Happens repeatedly → perception fades → belief fades → react repeatedly
- Something happens → healthy response

This process takes unconscious beliefs and transmutes them into conscious beliefs. A child's limited and hidden belief becomes challenged and it is a deliberate, purposeful, and strategic transformation into a sound adult belief. Over time, and true to the Principle of Rhythm, the sound and rational adult belief will eventually fade into the unconscious and operate positively for a lifetime.

When I first learned the basics of CBT, it was a relatively new therapy model. I was very impressed with its simple concepts and embraced its merits immediately. Not surprisingly, over the years CBT has become the therapeutic standard for therapists nationwide and has since established itself as the most effective therapy on the planet for most types of mental health challenges and addiction treatment. It is so simple that even the patients can use it once they learn the steps. Many behavioral health and treatment centers do, in fact, teach their patients a three-step or four-step system for do-it-yourself transmutations. (For a sample, see the Do-It-Yourself CBT worksheet at the end of this chapter.)

Doing it yourself is not always the best way, however. Finding the hidden unconscious belief is oftentimes pretty tricky. Since our core beliefs seem so natural and are ingrained in our very being, the owner of them tends to overlook what is obviously flawed. An outsider is much more likely to take notice of the unsoundness of a belief. A therapist can be helpful for discovering those beliefs.

CBT is in strict alignment with the philosophic principle that dates thousands of years ago. Truth shows itself one way or another. It is also another example of how spiritual/philosophic ideas are now being embraced by science.

There are a couple of issues of which to be aware. One is that we may not be as eager to let go of the old belief as one might think—but letting go is essential. Two, if we are aware of this ability to change, but our *will* to move forward is not there, then the discomfort actually increases. As we have covered, "letting go" is fairly important if we want to put our minds at ease.

The beauty of this transmutation process is that it is available to us at all times. It is not always easy, but it is available once we know how to do it. CBT is a prime consideration for making the jump from negative hidden unconscious belief scenarios to a higher level of positive conscious living that is purposefully integrated into our very being.

Refusing to Participate

The Principle of Rhythm paves the way for another way to create a favorable change. It has to do with the fact that humans have the freedom of choice. We can think outside of the human collective consciousness that says we have to endure the pain of life as it comes along. This human collective consciousness would have us believe that we are helpless against cycles that tend to repeat. After all, no one has changed the four seasons. No one has turned love into purple.

Thankfully, we can stand up to what seems as inevitable negativity—not from the physical plane, but from the mental plane.

With self-discipline we can basically *refuse* to participate in the *effects* of the cycle all the while the cycle continues. This denial of the effects is not a denial of the conditions. As the three initiates state it is just our way of **"rising above a thing and letting it pass beneath you."**

It is as if we bridge ourselves over the conditions of the troubling waters of our lives. It goes like this: The waters of a river flow calmly and quietly. But just as the seasons predict, the waters can become raging and wild according to cycles of nature. When we live from an unconscious plane, we are figuratively immersed in those waters. Inevitably, after enjoying the calmness of the relaxing waters for a period of time, the calm waters change to rough waters. We may get bounced around in the currents; pushed in all directions by the rushing waters; pulled down into the depths of the water. This is when life is paralyzing and scary.

> *The cycles of life will continue even as we take charge and rise above them with willful elevation of our minds from less consciousness to more consciousness. We can deny the influence that the back swing has over us.*

Instead of having panic or jumping into fear-based ego places mentally, we can use the poles of Unconscious and Conscious; we can allow the waters to rush on as we *will* ourselves to consciously build a mental bridge over those waters and take refuge on that higher level of consciousness. We would be on *the bridge over troubled waters*—to borrow from that famous song title (that borrowed from somewhere else).

This bridge over troubled waters works as related to our emotions. The grief, depression, or anger holds us down. We can, however, let those troubling feelings move beneath us as we *willingly* move our consciousness above it, on to a bridge of safety, of calmness, even of enthusiasm. We, in effect, *deny* the power that grief, depression, frustration, impatience, and such can have over us.

The bridge-over-troubled-waters process is akin to the notion of stepping into an Observer Self. The Observer Self is detached from the emotional upheaval that presents itself in life. We can *deliberately, willfully,* and *consciously* pull ourselves from the *emotional* strife of events and focus on the facts, truths, and rational aspects. This is a way of observing the events with a degree of detachment. It allows our observing conscious minds to be in charge in place of the reactionary emotional self. We are, in effect, observing the rough waters action while perched on the safety of a self-made mindful bridge. This is a far better place from which to make decisions. It creates security.

As stated by the Three Initiates: **"The Hermetic Master, or advanced student, polarizes himself at the desired pole and by a process akin to 'refusing' to participate in the backward swing . . . he stands firm in his polarized position, and allows the mental pendulum to swing back along his unconscious plane."**

A key aspect of this tool is that it is about the influence the Principle of Rhythm has over our minds. Things in life may be *emotionally* heading backward, but our *mental* state does not have to head backward. We can know a higher truth consciously and mindfully. For example, we can let the economic recession have its way, but at the same time not be mentally upset by it—therefore, not really being a part of it ourselves. You have heard of "mind over matter;" this is mind over perceptions—changing facts and emotional responses.

Law of Compensation

Another important aspect of the Principle of Rhythm has to do with what is called the Law of Compensation. There is a counterbalancing of things in life. As we know from the Principle of Rhythm, to whatever degree the pendulum swings to the right, it swings to the left. The Three Initiates stated this: **"The force with which a projectile is sent upward a mile is reproduced when the projectile returns to the earth on its return journey."**

We understand this in the physical world, but it also is true in the Spiritual and Mental planes. Since our focus is about finding true inner comfort consciously, I want to delve into this Law of Compensation with emphasis on mental planes. From the mental plane, we can understand the Law of Compensation from another direct quote of the Three Initiates of *The Kybalion*.

"The man who enjoys keenly, is subject to keen suffering; while he who feels but little pain is capable of feeling but little joy. The pig suffers but little mentally and enjoys but little—he is compensated."

The rule is that the capacity for pain and pleasure, in each individual, is balanced. It seems that we might not be able to enjoy life if we have the consciousness that says, "I am destined to suffer since I just experienced wonderful pleasure. I am trapped in an uncontrollable but predictable cycle." Who would want to experience outrageous joy, if, in fact, we know that we are on a cycle that will result in outrageous sorrow? And it does seem as if life happens that way sometimes. That rather pessimistic idea has its own compensation in the nature of things.

Negative to Positive Inclination

If you recall from the Principle of Polarity, the poles of polarity have a negative charge and a positive charge. This is in much the same manner as negative and positive magnetic poles. There is a natural tendency for positive vibration to overcome negative polarity vibration. We, as thinking and creative people, can and do manipulate, transform and transmute the rhythms of mental movement quite frequently—and often with painful results if not done mindfully. This is true for the individual person as well as for the mass consciousness of whole cultures.

The nature of the motion of polarity always has a way of overcoming negative by way of a positive movement. This is based on the fact that we have the freedom to choose; and choices are usually positive. With the *will* and *intention* to do so, we find contentment with a little mental alchemy. We can aim for the positive. While they may not be the exact things we had in mind, manifestations will be more to our liking.

Review Points

- Everything manifested in the Universe moves in a predictable way that can be both comfortable and less comfortable.
- "As above, so below; as below, so above" plays into the rhythm of life, and having this awareness allows for the use of helpful tools for handling the ebbs and flows of life.
- No matter what plane of life—mental, physical, or spiritual—we gain confidence in the predictability of movement.

- Even the perceived lack of control over the predictable changes of life and energy can be overcome with mental tools.
- The conscious and unconscious Mind has multiple tools for easing the pain of recurring changes and stuck ways of being—especially when using transformational tools (such as CBT).
- We do not have to participate in undesirable ebbs and tides of life when we utilize the mental bridge over troubled waters or simply refuse to participate emotionally.

Belief Transformation Exercise

See the "Do-It-Yourself CBT" belief transmutation worksheet and follow the directions above. Turn the book sideways and follow as numerically indicated on the worksheet. It is not necessary to use the worksheet itself since it is simple enough to draw the required eight boxes on your own paper as illustrated. From your own makeshift diagram, you can work out the steps on your own.

FINDING TRUE INNER COMFORT

Do-It-Yourself CBT

Start here, work your way down column.
Uncomfortable or Irrational Approach ➡

Transform by working down this column.
New Comfortable & Rational Approach ➡

Something Happens

The Same or Similar Events

Perception

Old, Limiting, or Child-like

New, Rational, and Adult-like

6. _____

EXAMPLE: *An old friend did not show up for my birthday party.*

7. _____

EXAMPLE: *There was something that got in the way of calling and arriving.*

1. _____

EXAMPLE: *A new friend did not show up at the park to play together.*

2. _____

EXAMPLE: *They think I am not good enough.*

BEING CONFIDENT

3. Meaning Example: *If I were good enough, everyone would keep their promises to me.* ___

Belief Example: *I'm not good enough.* ___

⬇ Old, Unsound or Child-like
⬆ New, Rational, and Adult-like

Meaning Becomes *Belief*

⬇ Old, Unsound or Child-like
⬆ New, Rational, and Adult-like

8. Meaning Example: (Mental Camera Check) *I don't really know what happened.* ___

Newly Chosen Belief Example: *I do my best and I am good enough.* ___

4. Example: *I feel hurt and angry and call the person a bunch of names on the phone and don't even listen for their excuse.* ___

⬇ Old Behavioral Reaction, Uncomfortable Emotions
⬆ Consciously Chosen Actions, Preferred Emotions

Response

9. End Here (New response is Initiated

Example: *I don't take it personally and feel concerned I call to see if my friend is okay.*

CHAPTER EIGHT

Being Creative

The **Principle of Cause and Effect** is also called the Principle of Causation. It addresses some really important aspects of the human experience. The impact on our ongoing desire for finding true inner comfort is richly revealed here. What is exciting about understanding the nature of Cause and Effect is that it gives us the chance to avoid and to rid ourselves of some of the most paralyzing ways of being that we have—helplessness, hopelessness, and magical thinking.

Often, we explain why things happen by saying, "This caused that." That explanation is *not* true because not *one* thing causes another thing to happen. Here is what the Principle of Cause and Effect explains.

> "Every Cause has its Effect; every Effect has its Cause; everything happens according to Law: Chance is but a name for Law not recognized: there are many planes of causation, but nothing escapes the Law."
>
> —THE KYBALION

The Principle explains that there is a cause for every effect and an effect for every cause. It maintains that there is no such thing as chance, that chance is merely a term indicating existing causes that are not yet recognized or perceived. Therefore, a cause is not the creator of an event. Instead of "this causes that," it is more accurately stated as "this" is the result of a series of causes going back so far that we do not see its beginning; and it does so according to the Laws of Nature. The notion of Cause and Effect is more accurately seen as Causes and Effects, with the beginning and end not known.

A Fallen Tree Limb

Let's look at a simple case in point. A tree limb falls in a storm. Before that, this limb was weakened by disease. The disease had its opportunity when a nest of insects fed on the tree itself in the hollow where a smaller limb had been cut away in a pruning event by a homeowner. It *appears* as if the storm made the dead limb fall. This was only a part of the picture.

We can see that it is not really accurate to say that the storm caused the limb to fall. We cannot, in fact, say the insects caused the limb to crash to the ground. And we cannot say that the homeowner's pruning caused the limb to fall. It was the chain of events going way beyond the latest and most dramatic of the causes and events—the storm. Most of the time, however, we would rashly conclude that the storm caused the limb to fall. We ignore the previous events or at least are unaware of them. We can see we don't really know the beginning of the causes and events. What we do know is that the causes lead to effects and the effects lead to causes. They are inseparable.

I am confining my exploration of Cause and Effect to ideas that interfere with human satisfaction and comfort. Great thinkers of the ages have before me tried to explain and understand Cause and Effect, which tend to address at least four basic concepts.

- Karma
- Luck and Chance
- Blessings and Grace
- Fate, Predestination, and Predetermination

Here, I limit and simplify our understanding of how each of the four notions interferes with finding the lasting pleasures of life. It is important to realize that we are talking about the out-there parts of our lives; the place of manifestations.

Karma

Karma has many different understandings across the world. I refer to Karma as related to the helpful or hurtful effects a person does in the world and their return to that person. This is "what goes around comes around." From an energetic standpoint this is in alignment with the notion that like attracts like in vibration and, therefore, it is pretty likely to show up in life with similar energy.

Familiar comments made in the Western world would have us understand that if I do something bad, I will have something bad happen to me in this life or the next (if we believe in reincarnation). Likewise, if I do acts of kindness I will somehow be rewarded with good things. Through our understanding of vibration, we can agree with this concept; however, it is not true in full. This simple cause-and-effect understanding of Karma is flawed in its oversimplification.

Cause and Effect is not a process of "This causes that," but actually is a chain of events that appears to have no beginning and to have no end. It is paradoxical in that it is called the Principle of Cause and Effect yet states that there is no Cause and Effect; instead it is causes and effects—as if they are one. They are One; one chain of events.

For our purposes here, an understanding of Karma would be better explained in general ideas. Rather than "this causes that" we would see it as a collection of *similar* deeds leads to many other deeds with related outcomes.

Many times, people accept the common understanding of Karma so simplistically that it appears to be a series of pay backs. It would seem that we can be victims of our own choices. This is not the way it really works.

Childlessness Caused Cancer?

For example, years ago a friend of mine made the statement that her choice to not have children as a young woman led to cervical cancer in her middle age. She had nagging thoughts that it was a woman's duty to have and raise children—something she never had a desire to do. Her idea was that being childless led to a Karma-type event—that payback of cancer. She explained it as "Because I did not use my female reproductive organs for having children, I was paid back by losing some of those organs."

A more accurate understanding of the cancer is really related to hundreds of unseen and unacknowledged happenings within her body. Some of those happenings took place even before she was born—tendencies carried in her DNA as passed down from generation to generation. There are many unknown causes that led to the effect of cancer.

When presented with this idea, my friend immediately related to the possibilities of many causes and stated that she has always been aware that cervical cancer "runs" in her family. This woman felt a great sense of relief when the notion of Karma was redefined with the understanding that no one thing causes another. Instead of childlessness causing cancer, she saw her cancer as the result of many causes, known and unknown.

Life unfolds in a long chain of causation, with an equal amount of effects that are impacted by our very thoughts, emotions, and behavior. We have a say in what happens.

Consider that Karma may just be a term for causation. Causation is based on a series of events, tendencies of vibration that include influences from Mental, Physical, and Spiritual energies. Karma is not the oversimplified notion of a payback or reward system of "This begets this or that." It might be more accurate to view Karma as outcomes whose origins seem known and whose channel is somewhat predictable.

Luck and Chance

Now we come to the notion of luck and chance. It is right to conclude from the Principle of Cause and Effect that luck or chance do not exist in truth. What does exist is our lack of perception about something—we fail to see how the odds of something happening as related to cause and effect.

The Principle of Cause and Effect reminds us that things do happen due to a chain of events, even when we don't see a cause. We are not aware of the full Principle of Cause and Effect wherein all the principles and Laws of Nature play into a given result. Key in this understanding is that our very thoughts are causes. Effects are manifestations. Yet such thoughts do not surface out of nowhere; they came about because of many perceptions, sights, understandings, and beliefs; a full creative process.

It is not an isolated thought that causes some effect. Instead, it is a lifetime of meanings and perceptions that cause conscious thoughts that, in turn, lead directly, and more often indirectly, to related manifestations.

Without our awareness of the principle we can be influenced in a negative manner by all the things happening around us even though they are engaging the natural chain of events. Having this awareness empowers us, as it debunks the notion of luck and chance. We can notice our own emotion-packed thoughts, knowing that we have beliefs that are strong and steadfast. One of the understandings about this awareness is that it saves us from being a victim of this or that as if one isolated cause is behind it—even if we label it bad luck. We can choose to see ourselves as victims of distasteful events and conditions and call it bad luck. Or we can choose to keep in mind that our lives are in the midst of causes and effects.

Gambling and Chance

Gambling is big business. It relies on our belief in good luck and in somehow beating the odds. The truth of the matter is that the roll of the dice, the deal of the card, and the flip of the coin all have equal chances for any one outcome. A person can become addicted to the process of gambling after repeated wins and losses. We can get charged up by the excitement of the *idea* of winning big.

For many, this excitement turns ugly. Some people are no longer charged up by the excitement of winning; they are taken over by the need to win in order to fix the financial ruin of their family's life. In the end, problem gamblers devastate their and their family's lives because of the belief in beating the odds. In truth, the chances of the dice landing with the six face-up is just as good as it landing with the one face-up. It follows the Laws of Nature.

Blessings and Grace

The Principle of Cause and Effect also brings to mind what we commonly call blessings and grace—images of God making warm-hearted interventions on our behalf. This idea would have us operating outside the Laws of Nature; it is God having compassion with our situations and somehow interrupting the Laws of Nature that we perceive as negative and replacing it with positive. God and the energies of Divinity can and will, in the process of helping us along in our growth, work within the laws that operate in all planes of existence—spiritual, physical, and mental. These "invisibles," as I call them with affection, do not operate outside the laws of the Universe just because we need a favor, or we behave properly, or we pray in the certain manner.

Blessings and grace from God are the pleasant and sometimes unexpected outcomes of cause and effect that are the result of a chain of thoughts and actions that operate within the Laws of Nature.

We see that those situations that we attribute to being a blessing or within God's grace are related to our alignment with the Laws of Nature, the laws of the Universe, and of God. Such laws do not play favorites. God acts according to Laws—many of which are presented in the seven principles of *The Kybalion*.

What we call blessings and grace from God are not what are commonly understood. Blessings and grace come about when our thinking and behavior *align* with The Laws of Nature and higher vibrations of God. We have a choice to be in alignment or not. These ideas are found in *The Kybalion* and the Bible and many other inspired and scientific texts. Being in alignment with God's natural ways means we are operating within the very vibrations of what we call grace. Getting into alignment with the ways of God is comforting in and of itself.

When we don't feel as if God is blessing us with some form of grace, we can become negative, resentful, and discouraged. In truth, we all have the same opportunity to experience grace if we only decide to put into motion a series of causes and effects that are bound by the Laws of Nature to reward us with pleasing conditions. Here, we can be the creative cause in the Cause vibration. In an automatic way, the Effect vibration is higher because of our purposeful effort to have more pleasing energy. The pleasing energy is, as we recall, the vibrations closest to those of our Creator.

In this way, we engage in life on a different level. We engage as cocreators with God. We cocreate by living our lives in the awareness that we are consciously and unconsciously contributing a lot of causes that do impact the nature of the effects in our lives. We are *being* closer to our Higher Power. This is being in alignment with those things that will make us aware of love, joy, and peace. *The Kybalion* authors state this: **"Knowing the rules of the game, Masters rise above the plane of material life, and placing themselves in touch with the higher power of their nature, dominate their own mood, characters, qualities, and polarity, as well as the environment**

surrounding them and thus become Movers in the game, instead of Pawns—Causes instead of Effects."

If we *consciously* become the movers of the game of life, we see an increase in pleasurable effects and manifestations. We can call those effects blessings and grace, but, in fact, we are simply being in alignment with God's higher vibrations. Referring to the Life Source illustration, it would be living in the energy inside the Sun—the love, peace, harmony, and joy area. When we live consciously with the knowledge that we are part of natural cause and effect instead of pawns of them, we will automatically feel blessed and full of grace. It is not that we earn it. It is that we step into that which is already there inside us. If we feel a lack of grace and blessing, we should, indeed, be taking a look at where we are focused in life—in the inner energy or *out-there*. With this response, we can step into a different energy instead of complaining about our Higher Power's apparent absence. I say *apparent* because those inner energies are always there when we want them.

Fate, Predestination, and Predetermination

Very controversial is the notion of fate, or what *The Kybalion* calls Determination. Is there such a thing or not? The Three Initiates state this: **"Neither side of the controversy is entirely right—in fact, both sides are partially right, according to the Hermetic teachings. The Principle of Polarity shows that both are but Half-Truths—the opposing poles of Truth."**

It certainly seems to be a gray area. Many people have a mind-set that accepts fate as Truth with various degrees of free will that can alter that fate. Some believe that our souls determine our fate; and that is that. Others believe that God determines our fate. Very common is the idea that a certain life event "seals our fate." All these ideas have the notion that life events and conditions are determined beforehand—are predetermined.

The Lesson of the Bicyclists

Years ago, I was director of a large social services agency in Florida. Part of my duties were to oversee the homeless shelter and assist the manager of it in its operations.

One day, the manager of the homeless shelter came to me with an issue related to a man who was staying in the shelter. The manager, who was very loving and compassionate, was at his wits' end in dealing with the wheelchair-bound man and the frustrated shelter staff.

He asked me to talk with the man in hopes of changing his very unpleasant disposition. Arriving at my office in his wheelchair, with his atrophied legs folded neatly in their assigned footrests, the man began to complain about everything. He was a very negative person who clearly saw himself as entitled to having all his demands met because of his physical limitations.

Being homeless and confined to a wheelchair is admittedly problematic. I acknowledged his situation and attempted to guide the man into thinking more positively. He was unwilling to go in that direction. I returned the man to the shelter with the intention of addressing the issue with the staff the next day. My hope was to change *their* perception since we could not change our guest's.

Driving home, I encountered dozens of bicyclists pedaling in the bike lane, spilling into the automobile lane—as they often did. I found my opportunity to pass the bikers and began the careful process. As I was overtaking the pedaling bikers, I happened

BEING CREATIVE

to glance to my right. What I saw created an instant emotional response in me.

In the middle of the pack of healthy and vibrant-looking bicyclists were six young men with withered-looking legs tucked under their bodies, pedaling mechanically altered bikes with their strong-looking arms. The altered bikes carried men whose faces showed a mixture of joy and freedom. I had a sense of awe as their determination to remain in the middle of the pack propelled them to work their arms as hard as needed to keep up with the rest of the group.

What I saw were men that would not be stopped by their physical limitations. I instantly thought of the wheelchair-bound man in my office who had just minutes before presented himself as helpless and victimized by life.

I thought of the huge contrast: these determined and inspiring bicyclists in contrast to the defeated man in my office. The bikers would not let their limitations lead to what others might see as a fate of giving up their love of bicycling. The man in the wheelchair at the homeless shelter was a victim of some crippling fate that *existed in his mind*.

Fate with Flexibility

This story makes my point about the flexibility of fate. All those men could live the fate of a small and limited life. They have the choice to tap into the flexibility of cause and effect. We can accept what seems the inevitable, or we can do something purposeful—use creative thinking that stimulates a series of causes and a collection of seemingly less likely end results. To me, this dispels the notion of our traditional use of the word "fate."

Being handicapped and acting limited is likely the road most traveled by those who lose the use of their legs or other parts of their bodies. But it is not a fate unless accepted as such. Less traveled, but far more empowering, is the creative road of determination. It is a victor's life as a cocreator.

Those powerful bikers changed their thinking, outlooks, and intentions along the way. Perhaps, without using any real knowledge of the Principle of Cause and Effect, they used its benefits nonetheless. Unlike predestination, fate, or destiny, a person's will to rise above her or his situation allows free will to engage in the creative self-determination in life. Consider these so-called limitations:

- Poor vision or blindness. Look at Helen Keller—deaf and blind she saw and shared way beyond what anyone can physically see.
- Ongoing health challenges. Consider Stephen Hawking—a genius whose body could have limited his very thinking, yet it did not.
- Being born into poverty. Think about Oprah Winfrey, a woman who defies all odds to become a modern-day messenger of love and kindness, at the same time becoming one of the richest (in more ways than one) women on Earth.
- Being raised by an addicted parent. Reflect on the countless success stories of clean and sober adults raised by abusive alcoholics.
- We all have heard of the countless "medical miracles" wherein patients are told they will never walk again, and not only walk but also dance; or they are told they will not live beyond ten years of age but live well into adulthood; and dozens of other limiting forecasts being overridden by peoples' determination to defy those predictions as cocreators of an improved alternative ending.

Each of these and many other examples carry with them certain "fated" outcomes. Or not. Most of the time, people are operating in the dark. There are certain things that are part of patterns in life. Like the pendulum, life progresses on a predictable course. And yet, we know that we can alter those so-called "predetermined" directions. This means that what we call fate and predetermination are not only flexible—but also they are workable. We simply have to use our God-given ability to create our own causes, which, in turn, will result in effects that are not fixed. It is tapping into the Inner Self of our being instead of resigning ourselves to out-there, ego-related fates.

"I guess it was not meant to be."

Many of us make that statement. We say it for the purpose of dismissing a disappointing event. It takes the responsibility of the event from us and puts it in a predetermined outcome of which we have no advanced knowledge. For example, we like the idea that we did not cause the job interview to result in not being hired. Let's blame it on the alignment of the stars. If pressed, however, we would admit that our responses in the interview may have been poor, and the responses of other candidates may have been quite good.

Cause and effect are present. Whether we like it or not, we have a hand in everything that presents itself to us. Not accepting this truth makes us sad victims of our own blaming thoughts. Accepting this truth does empower us. There is restoration of our being in that awareness.

Supposed To

Some of us say that "it's not in the cards" because we sincerely believe in some form of "set-in-stone" script in life. These types of statements indicate some belief in the idea that life is fair, or should be, and when it is not, we cry, "Foul." At times in our lives, we might say, "This was not supposed to happen." Often this is said because we did not see it coming. Maybe we say it because we have projected other outcomes firmly in our minds.

Young children are not supposed to die before their parents. When this happens, it is a hard pill to swallow. Indeed, a child's death seems unthinkable and tragic beyond belief for the parents. Conclusions based on the Principle of Cause and Effect would explain such heartbreaking events in a rather cold and detached manner. A long collection of causes has effects and manifestations that become causes of their own. This cause-and-effect process continues until an "accident" or illness comes about, seemingly out of nowhere. It can and does go against what we always expected of life.

What God Wants?

Callous as it seems, a child's unexpected and unwanted death comes down to a feeling of "that should *not* happen." The consequences may be more than anyone is willing to emotionally and logically tolerate. At these times we can hear ourselves say something like, "It must be what God wants." Or "Why did God allow this to happen?"

Putting God into the picture is a good idea, since everything is the Creator. The All has all in It, so putting God in a place of tragedy seems logical and warranted. The problem with statements such as "It must be what God wants" is that it assumes that God operates in such ways. Assuming God wants something is borrowing from a human characteristic. People want things. The All is not in need of anything, since it is all and has all already. To be more accurate, God just *is*.

Our Source is the Law with a capital letter L. The Law is a collection of all the laws and principles of life that operate with or without our input, desires, and expectations. Another way to view this is as "The Way." The Way is not fate. The Way is just the natural process of what is to come if the causes and effects continue as they are. The Way includes the law of causation—the Principle of Cause and Effect. Being in alignment with the nature of causes and effects is being in alignment with God. Being in this orientation does allow us to use the natural process of choices to create our own stream of causes, which, in turn, steers our lives in different directions.

Back to our very uncomfortable example, a child's life ends because of an endless process of causes and effects impacted in that way. We have a right to feel the gut-wrenching grief associated with a child's death, but to point blame is pointless. Accepting this uncommon idea of no blame has its own satisfaction.

Listening and Looking for Signs

Important to the idea of being in alignment with the Laws of Nature is our ability to look for signs. Many of us do, in fact, look for signs along the way. In a short listing, we look to see if we are supposed to go in this direction, make this choice, have this thing, or achieve this deed.

Being in alignment with God can be compared to canoeing in a river. It is not a hard journey if I stay in the river, or at least be near it; and go with the flow of the river instead of paddling upstream. I can be mindful of the ability to use the river's current to my advantage. In life, I can find signs that lead to the river. Some people call this listening to life.

What is right for us? It is being in alignment with the path that is in harmony with our Source. It is *using* the Laws of Nature and universe instead of fighting those comforting movements. We get to choose the temporary out-there things or the lasting inner things. When we listen to life's messages, we increase our chances of seeing what is right for us.

Masters of Our Fate

Whether we are aware of it or not, it is safe to say that each and every one of us is the master of our own fate. If you critically think about it, this means that fate is simply a term that accepts the idea that certain things are likely to happen if no particular new thoughts are introduced. That we can change our thoughts and therefore change the outcome of what might seem resolute and "fateful" is the conscious approach.

As with many spiritually studied people, I tend to believe in a mixture of free will and flexible fate. In this line of thinking, our souls predetermine a general life-plan before we are even born. From this understanding, we have a Divine opportunity to experience life lessons through sometimes difficult situations. This sets the stage for scenarios in life by which we can experience what the soul seeks to learn more deeply. Blended into this is the notion that our own free will can veer off course, but the same lessons will be presented to us in different guises. Free will does allow for many of us to never learn the lesson during a lifetime.

Rather than destiny being something set in stone by unseen factors in the stars, we are in charge of our own destiny. It is a journey of perception and cocreation.

Review Points

- There is no one cause and effect—it is, instead, an infinite number of causes and effects that lead from one to the other as One. Blaming is a counter-creative process as a result.
- Instead of a "this caused that" mentality, the endless series of related positive or negative cause-and-effect events makes up what is commonly called Karma.
- Chance and luck are terms used in explaining effects we do not perceive. They are not real, but our lives feel hopeless if we believe in these manifestations.
- We have the power to cocreate our own realities that form within our endless stream of similarly related cause and effect energies.
- Blessings and grace from God are the pleasant and unexpected outcomes of cause-and-effect that are the direct and indirect results of our choices. We are simply reaping the rewards of being in alignment with God's higher vibrations.
- Each one of us is a key part of the process of cause and effect and therefore we cocreate our lives within a flexible course of possibilities, not a rigid predestination or fate.

Affirmative Prayer

There is One Power and Source.

And I am One with It.

I affirm an understanding that life is flexible and workable.

Life is led by endless causes and effects.

I know that I have a say in causes and effects.

I have the ability to mold my life by use of the power of my own intentions, perceptions, and beliefs.

I live in harmony with the natural Laws of the Universe so that life feels like a blessing, even when it feels less comfortable.

Living consciously, I am in alignment with that which is in my best interest.

It is with gratitude and humility that I interact with the world,

And I reap the benefits of that by experiencing love, peace, and joy every day.

In every action it is my intention that love, peace, and joy not only are my experience, but also a shared experience with everyone that I encounter.

I release any and all doubts and beliefs that are in conflict with these words.

It is so, and so it is.

CHAPTER NINE

Being Authentic

*E*ach of us has suffered at least some type of pain to varying degrees. One primary brand of pain is caused in large part by gender imbalances. It results in our inability to be authentically expressive.

In the quest for finding true inner comfort, and avoiding the difficulties associated with looking for comfort out-there in the physical world, we have to be authentic. That includes the notion of coming from a place of "being" rather than "doing."

As related to the **Principle of Gender,** we have to accept ourselves as having *both* Masculine and Feminine energies. Failing to accept both Masculine and Feminine energies in our perceptions, thoughts, and beliefs results in behavior that is out of balance. Out-of-balance behavior confounds our expressive and creative processes.

The good news is that we can correct gender imbalance. We do this by way of achieving authenticity. This genuineness-obtaining process is about affirming a greater truth of our creative being. That greater truth is directly related to understanding the nature of gender as presented by the seventh axiom. The Principle of Gender states:

> "Gender is in everything: everything has its Masculine and Feminine Principles. Gender manifests on planes."
> —THE KYBALION

Gender Is Not the Same as Sex

These distinctions are not the conventional concepts we have learned. There are a few clarifications that need to be made about the term gender, especially as used in the Principle of Gender. Without making real distinctions about the two terms, gender and sex, there is a good chance of becoming confused by the principle itself.

The word Gender comes from a Latin root that means "to beget; to procreate; to generate; to create; to produce." From this understanding we can see that gender has a broad base.

Sex, on the other hand, is really about the distinctions between living things that are labeled as male and female. Sex relates to physical-plane aspects of procreation. It does not include the Spiritual and Mental planes in the manner that gender does.

The Nature of The All

The Principle of Gender, which seeks to explain one of the key original aspects of our Higher Power, is related to the creative process itself. If we recall, all things are vibration energy. As a result, we have to look at creativity as about the nature of vibration and movement. Vibration and movement are fundamental to God and, therefore, all things. Accepting our true nature as vibration-based beings primes us to accept that both Feminine and Masculine vibrations are present in us all.

That means that our creative and expressive selves require an acceptance of who we are *as* we are. Accepting our authentic self is tricky business. It is complicated and full of barriers and uncomfortable side steps. Embracing our true selves is about accepting something that for most of us is elusive; the perplexing issue of "Who am I?"

The Root of Most Human Suffering

Gender imbalance is so basic and confounding that many professionals in the field of psychology believe it to be at the root of most human suffering. Some anguish may be a quiet and insidious pain of just trying to be the best man or woman—as defined by a particular society. One society's rules about what is manly or ladylike may not fit a particular individual. A person may allow that notion to become a problem in order to feel accepted. Even more problematic, there are societies and cultural norms that believe their way is the *only* acceptable way. People operating outside of that "norm" become recipients of condemnation.

Some suffering is more pronounced, such as from sexual orientation, gender orientation, and other rejection related to homophobia. We can even consider the scenario of a heterosexual who dances to his or her own tune. They can become the victim of bullying, isolation, rejection, and humiliation if perceived as not strictly stereotypical "all boy" or "girly girl." Cringe-worthy terms.

Another aspect of gender rejection appears to push the individual in a dual comfort-seeking effort. For instance, many people desperately seek to feel a sense of belonging and acceptance at any cost. They may somehow find acceptance with other people who exaggerate their own masculine-dominance energy. When these individuals get together, they get a false sense of belonging and a real sense of protection. Examples of this sort of exaggerated power-seeking include youth attraction to gang affiliation and the radicalism of individuals from minority groups who become attracted to terrorism. These human efforts are based on man's insidious or blatant battle with his own masculine and feminine identities.

The diagram on the following page may help in wrapping your mind around the understanding of the principle's energy-based concepts of Feminine and Masculine purposes in life.

The struggle to prove oneself takes on huge intensity within each individual person. It gets even more intense and emotional when combined with religious ideals and dogma as a group, movement, or organization. Consider that an organization like the KKK, which promotes a collection of people united for segregation by race, is in part fueled by gender imbalances. Along with fear of change, it is fear of differences; a failure to accept that all peoples of all types are different expressions of one human race. This is opposite of our desire to be accepted as we are.

The Masculine principle is always in the direction of giving out or expressing. The Feminine principle is always in the direction of receiving impressions. It has a much more varied field of operation than the Masculine. The Feminine has strength as it conducts the work of generating new thoughts, concepts, and ideas, including the work of the imagination.

Taking a look at the issue of authenticity as it applies here, we see that being real cannot take place if the balance between masculine

PRINCIPLE OF GENDER DISTINCTIONS

Masculine Gender Characteristics	Feminine Gender Characteristics
Masculine found in all things, including the female of species.	Feminine is found in all things, including the male of species
Bonds with feminine energy to catalyze for creation—explains cocreation.	Bonds with masculine energy to catalyze for creation—explains cocreation.
Energy moves outward.	Energy draws inward.
Energies are called Positive because of positive electric flow.	Energies are called Negative or Cathode because of negative electric flow.
Energies tend to project, give out, express, and act from operations of "will."	Energies are receptive, nurture, receive impressions, including imagination.
Tendency is in the direction of giving out and/or expressing.	Tendency is in the direction of receiving impressions.
Too much masculine energy (doing too much at the expense of receiving, overly competitive, having too much stress) can result in reduced ability to feel spirit flow.	Too much feminine energy can result in a passive personality, observing life rather than acting upon or expressing ideas and thoughts.
Is one half of the dual minds—masculine energy called "conscious."	Is one half of the dual minds—feminine energy called "unconscious."
Contents itself with the work of "Will," whose energy helps prompt the feminine into developing original mental creations—instead of relying on outside impressions.	Conducts the work of new thoughts, ideas, concepts, including the work of the imagination.

energy and feminine energy is not allowed to flow. When we keep in mind that everything we do is about begetting, procreating, generating, creating, and producing, it stands to reason that anything that we devalue, deny, or otherwise find unacceptable in ourselves causes uneasiness—small and large. This results in being unhappy due to having a poor perception of our own being.

We can conclude that our tendency for inauthentic ways is related to our egos trying to somehow make creative negative self-perceptions appear acceptable. Unfortunately, most of us find temporary and artificial out-there ways to get comfort and yet we expect permanent comfort. This is our basic set-up for looking out-there for comfort.

So, if I am high on marijuana, for example, I am okay with how I perceive myself and how I think you perceive me. The chemical interaction with my brain allows for that. With an altered mind, I am okay with how I perceive you, even though my perception is distorted by the chemicals. As long as I am not reminded of the fact that I am accepting you with an altered mind, then I am okay with my perception as if it were fact-based. And even if I am reminded of it, I can deny it. It is no wonder that daily smoking of marijuana has become a satisfactory, inauthentic way of living for so many. It seems as if it is a reasonable life, but it does limit one's life and it is a life that is not based on what is true.

We Are Taught Lies

A lot of the deceptions we are taught are related to our sexual identities. This is so because we align with gender identities as part of our very being. Society helps us be confused by our gender and sexual identity expressions by telling us false facts. Author Don Miguel Ruiz describes what he calls "human domestication" in his book *The Four Agreements*. In a beautiful way, he explains that human domestication comes about from the imposed rules and values of our family and society. His conclusions are that we do not usually have the chance to decide on our biased childhood beliefs, since they are forced upon us. The biases of our forefathers and foremothers are falsehoods told, not out of malice, but as tradition. These lies tell us *how* we are supposed to feel and behave as based on society norms. Nowhere is that truer than handed-down thoughts, perceptions, and beliefs associated with gender and sexuality.

In considering just a few common biases, we see how these become the seeds of untruths. In Western society, boys are not given dolls to play with and girls are not given toy army men to play with. The typical instructions by their families are that boys should not feel sad and show tears; and girls are told they will not be seen as womanly if they serve in the armed forces.

What Is the Truth?

The Truth is we are beings with a creative vibration. It is our very essence. The creative process occurs because of vibration and intention. From the standpoint of the productive process, intention has to do with gender. Not only does society not inform us of this beautiful fact, it teaches us the opposite. We are taught that masculine (male) and feminine (female) are opposing ideas that are exclusive to one another. This is not true. We, as sexual beings, are, in truth, equipped with both feminine and masculine gender qualities. Thus, we can procreate sexually within the physical sexual process as male or female; *and* we can create physically, mentally, and spiritually from interactions of our masculine and feminine gender aspects.

Within each of us are the roles of the gender energy. A never-ending process of procreation, reproduction, and creation is the result of the interactions of Masculine Vibration and Feminine Vibration. Each gender has its own "duties," and they are dependent on each other for harmony of effort.

Herein is the crux of authenticity. It seems that humans, as conditioned by society, are not always comfortable with the presence and expression of *both* Masculine and Feminine aspects. In trying to be more at ease, we end up denying, defending, stifling, or otherwise putting the balance and harmony of the creative process in turmoil. We create the imbalance ourselves. We have society's biases (lies) to thank for that. The usual imbalance is so commonplace that it seems normal.

Lack of Authenticity Is Crippling

This absence of balance and harmony can be seen in people's lives as a reduction in being real and being free. This flies in the face of our most inner urges; we just want to be ourselves—free of having to defend or deny any aspect of our being. Each one of us has had inner turmoil because of certain self-defenses and self-denial about our Feminine and Masculine energies; therefore, resulting in conflict about our expression and creative process. By accepting lies about gender, we feel that we must choose one or the other. Failing to accept that we all have Masculine and Feminine energies within us automatically kills authenticity.

A lack of authenticity shows up in hundreds of ways. But the archetypes are familiar for denial and defense:

- We have the tendency to hide certain aspects of ourselves that we perceive as unacceptable as per our gender. A girl is reluctant to show off her athletic abilities. A gifted medic in the armed services is reluctant to use those rewarding nursing skills outside the armed forces in a community hospital where he will not be a nurse, but a "male nurse."
- We may exaggerate certain aspects of ourselves that we perceive as unacceptable. A boy who is made aware of his "weak" ways believes being forceful and controlling is a manly way to be and tends to bully other kids.
- We have the tendency to pretend to be one way, when in fact we are another way. This could take the form of taking on roles, personas, and images that move the focus off gender-related aspects of us. A lesbian woman marries a man because that somehow proves that she is heterosexual. This is important to her because she accepted the lie that homosexuality is less than acceptable due to specific untrue "facts."
- We may start to overly embrace positive gender qualities of life that are external in nature. These are ego-driven qualities and include our roles as super-dad or super-mom, perfect son or daughter, all-American athlete and scores of other gender-biased roles and labels.
- We may accept negative characteristics to the point that we become crippled and stuck in such titles as innocent victim, a no-good bum, a failure in life, someone going nowhere,

and many others. While these may not be gender-based, they often are gender-shaming in orientation.

It Starts with Gender Imbalances

For the purpose of illustration, I will use the most extreme form of comfort-seeking—addiction. The reason for using mind-altering drugs, including alcohol, oftentimes begins with being uncomfortable with some aspect that the person perceives in his or her self. The perception is most often gender related even if disguised.

Let's say the person finds a drug or group of drugs that somehow temporarily take the discomfort away. The discomfort is likely related to not measuring up to "acceptable" womanhood or manhood. It often leads to exaggerated behaviors. The drugs alter the person's experience in life. What they see about themselves and about life is altered (reduced, enhanced, twisted)—probably favorably at first. What other people see in the drug user is an altered person—not the real person. The interactions between the drug-using person and the others are not authentic. They may think they like each other or detest each other, but, in fact, they don't even know each other.

Lives caught up in this type of interaction are destined to suffer from problems. The lack of authenticity is at the core of the relationships—including the relationship that the drug user has with his or her Inner Self. This is the nature of imbalances of gender energy.

I restate: The reason that the drug user was uncomfortable with his or her self is primarily rooted in one core aspect of life—gender. How so? Remember that gender, as a defined word, comes from the meaning "to beget; to procreate; to generate; to create; to produce." *Everything* begins with creativity and, therefore, Masculine and

Feminine genders. Included in the creative processes are such things as school grades and projects, children, careers, artistic endeavors, achieving success, and academic pursuits, and the list goes on. If we are uncomfortable about anything related to ourselves, we can trace it back to being distressed with something related to those aspects. We go about *creating* in all sorts of ways; expressing in fantastic diversity. All are subject to potential twistedness.

Much to our discomfort, we often experience what we see as setbacks. Each of us has our own real and perceived setbacks. Somehow, we see that we are not measuring up. Our own perception is difficult. This is perhaps based on negative input from others—a perception that we mistakenly accept as true. Since we know that "It is as we believe," despite the real Truth, our personal truth becomes the truth of our lives. In other words, our own truth might as well be the Truth even though it is a lie. The lie tells us to shut down, recoil, hide, pretend, exaggerate, or tell stories. It prevents us from being our true selves. It prevents creativity and therefore authenticity.

Battle of the Sexes

The battle of the sexes begins before birth. It is really a battle of the genders, as well. Will the baby be a girl or boy? Parents secretly have their preferences. After birth, we are treated one way or another largely depending on our gender. Boys are to be one way. Girls are to be another way. If either fails to measure up to perceived norms, then there are uncomfortable consequences from societal pressures.

Even so, if that nonconforming child were to be uprooted and placed in a different society, she or he might very well fit in just the way she or he is. The values placed in gender roles, rules, and stereotypes are based on learned, accepted, and arbitrary ideas that are passed on from generation to generation depending on the specific environment. The most uncomfortable things we experience in life include rejection and nonacceptance—that feeling of not being okay. To feel as if we are not acceptable the way we are is the basis of most inner conflicts, which, then, lead to outer conflicts.

When we are first discovered, we are thought of as a fetus; a genderless, sexless life-form that is human. In Truth, we are already full of sexual and gender energies. The next question is, "Is it a boy or a girl?" There the duality begins. The contrasts. The competitiveness. The measuring up. The vibration is full of tension. It begins with those identity issues. In the real world, we all have ideas of what it is to be a man; and to be a woman.

With distorted perceptions, we do not measure up to the feminine and masculine ideas that people give us, and we do not measure up to the sex and gender roles we give ourselves.

In our minds, our fathers fall short on the manhood scales. Our mothers were too much this way or that way to be considered woman of the year. Our partners in life do not measure up either. This might explain why so many of us have short-lived partnerships. It seems that our failure to measure up never ends. We don't accept others because they are not the kind of man or woman they *should* be, and we don't accept ourselves because we know or believe that we don't measure up either. This is a dis-eased way of living.

Seeking true inner comfort—the process of looking inside rather than out-there for relief—leads us to a possible way of achieving real comfort as related to authenticity. It is about feeling it is okay to just be—free to be. The caveat is it will not really happen unless the gender energy is in balance.

One way off of this treadmill is to throw out the old traditional measuring stick. Since most of us have sexual identities as male or female, we forget that we have *both* genders from an energetic understanding. The challenge is to know who we *are* as beings—not on ideas related to what we *do*. Instead, we can accept that we are what we are based on the inside stuff. If we refer to the Life Source illustration, we can see that we are love, peace, and joy at the very core. This is contrary to what we are often taught, which are aspects of our outer world—the out-there aspects depicted in the Sun's rays of the illustration.

All too often, we fail to embrace the inside in favor of embracing only what is seen on the outside. This includes embracing the things that we beget, produce, create, procreate, and so forth. Failing to embrace the energies found *inside* ourselves, we will keep wondering who we are—who we really are. Our identities will remain clouded by the lies, half-truths, and distortions of what people tell us: what we tell ourselves as related to what we do, what our labels are, and outer appearances. Even more unsettling is the fact that those out-there identities are, by their very nature, constantly changing.

When we can embrace ourselves, we can embrace everyone else. This is a gift we give ourselves by accepting our inner selves. The stereotyping of people by gender only creates a feeling of separation. It makes for the notion that differences are not acceptable. Those ideas lead to depression, bullying, divorce, conflicts, and wars which are based on ideas that are not even true. It tends to lead us into ways of seeing ourselves as unacceptable—which leads to inauthentic living. We could instead be honoring those differences.

Achieving Gender Balance

It is said that there must be a balance in these two creative forces. Without the Feminine, the Masculine is apt to act with little to no restraint, order, or reason. This results in chaos. Masculine imbalance could bring lack of restraint that leads to fighting and lack of order. These lead to chaos of the mind, of the life, of society and culture. It also promotes a lack of reason and rationality. As an aspect of problem comfort-seeking, it leads into addictive, repetitive, and compulsive behaviors with the potential for violent controlling actions. Both men and women find themselves in this dis-eased and somewhat ugly state.

Perhaps not as ugly, but just as significant is the Feminine imbalance. If Feminine energy, which is critical to creativity, is not in balance with Masculine energy the creative process is apt to reflect on things too much and often fail to manifest. This stagnation only comes about because it needs the Masculine to balance it. We can see that this could lead to lack of productivity in life. Letting things happen, living as a victim, and other stagnation would be the result in life—as a person and collectively as nations. It is not just women that slip into this depressing place; the strength of Feminine energy must be in balance within both men and women in order for real creativity to take place.

With both the Masculine and Feminine working in conjunction, there is mindfulness action that breeds success. This points out that both the Feminine and the Masculine fulfill each other. There must be a harmony between the Masculine and Feminine for us to find serenity. So even though peace is found inside us naturally, we will not feel it and become aware of its presence if our gender energies are out of balance.

The balance between Masculine and Feminine energy actually creates harmony, which allows for feelings that promote authenticity. From this place, we feel no reason to be anything that we are not; no altered selves. This, of course, is the very foundation for finding true inner comfort—Feminine and Masculine energies working together in harmony. In an ideal sense, our very being is accepted just as it is. We are then free to be spontaneous.

Imagine being able to accept all aspects of your gender energies without judgment. There is no needless competition. There is no need to stereotype. There is no need to act a certain way. We don't have to be a certain way to be acceptable, so there are no judgments and expectations. There is no preference for one or the other.

You would be free to be your own creative self without regard to what people judge as related to roles and the actions related to masculine and feminine. You would not be afraid to be yourself. This freedom to be you is liberating to the highest degree. It allows you to be as creative as you want. It permits your Masculine "will" to impregnate your Feminine receptive creative manifestations.

The real Self is not the stereotypes. In the realm of the Divine, we are not our roles. We are not our thoughts, our feelings, or our beliefs. We are not our labels of man or woman or homosexual, bisexual, transsexual, or heterosexual. We are not our job titles. We are not our personal histories—stories of various dramas that result in terms such as criminals, addicts, victims, predators, divorcées, troublemakers, or even less controversial such terms as Republicans, Democrats, protesters, mothers, fathers, and so on.

We often hear that we are spiritual beings having a human experience. From the gender-energy understanding, we get a better view of that spiritual being. As spiritual beings, we are forces of energy that vibrate in order to create, and we use Masculine energy combined with Feminine energy for the purpose of perpetuating the internal spirit life. As human beings, we are forces of mental energy that vibrate in order to create and use both Masculine and Feminine energies in conjunction with each other. The same is said of our physical plane of life, which uses Masculine and Feminine energy to create.

In summary, gender is energy and it manifests in everything. Sex, gender roles, sexual identity, and sexual orientation are only parts of the creative process. Even grander still, gender is about creating a balance in Feminine and Masculine energies so that we can "... beget; procreate; generate; create; and produce...." in everyday living.

Gender is manifested as the Masculine and Feminine principles, and manifests itself mentally, physically, and spiritually. It wants to be in harmony and balance. That begins with our willingness to allow the energies to act in the ways in which they are inclined to act. This allows us to be authentic and without fear.

It is important for you to examine your own fears as related to your Masculine and Feminine qualities. Expressing yourself freely and creating in your life as fully as possible is what we call Divine Right Action. This is the road to feeling liberated enough to just be. Just *be*; and see that what you create is beautiful.

Review Points

- As sexual beings, we are equipped with both Feminine and Masculine gender qualities. We procreate sexually—with our physical sexual process—as male or female; and we cocreate

physically, mentally, and spiritually from interactions of our Masculine and Feminine gender aspects.
- Accepting ourselves as creative beings allows for true authenticity and freedom. Everything we do is about begetting, procreating, generating, creating, and producing. As a result, we want to avoid thoughts and behaviors that tend to devalue, deny, or otherwise reject parts of ourselves.
- When we accept lies about gender, we feel that we must choose one or the other. Failing to accept that we all have Masculine and Feminine energies within us kills authenticity.
- Masculine imbalance could bring lack of restraint that leads to fighting and lack of order. This leads to chaos of the mind, of the life, of society and culture. It also promotes a lack of reason and rationality, which often leads to addictive, repetitive, and compulsive behaviors. Feminine energy imbalance leads one to constantly reflect and fail to actually do anything, resulting in stagnation. Achieving balance is by accepting within your very being the fact that you have both Feminine and Masculine energies and by allowing them equal time to create.
- Equal acceptance of both Masculine and Feminine energy begins with our willingness to allow the energies to act in the ways in which they are inclined to act. This allows us to be authentic, which is the most satisfying state of being there is.

Affirmative Prayer

Incorporating many of the ideas put forth in all the presented chapters, you can choose one, some or all of the various affirmations (that are shown in bulleted italics) below. Take your chosen italicized affirmations and sandwich them in-between beginning and ending statements that are in bold font.

There is one creative force that we know as God and many other terms.

I am one with that creative force, having the power and creativity within my own experience, and I embrace both my masculine and feminine energies.

- *I choose to use my mind for creative purposes and healing power.*
- *I know that I am part of the cocreative process of unlimited causes and resulting effects, including the masculine will and the feminine manifest.*
- *I accept change as fundamental to life and no longer resist change.*
- *I have the power to change my perception.*
- *I accept that cause and effect create the truth of "becoming" wherein I can "let things be" because all things pass.*
- *I am aware that good and comfort are already in my physical, spiritual, and mental vibrations.*
- *I am free to be my true self because of my acceptance of my true nature as spiritual and as cocreative.*
- *I consciously take responsibility for my life, setting the highest of intentions so that I always do my best in thought and action.*
- *I now let go of whatever I am clinging onto; releasing the vibration of now for the vibration of the next now; being unattached by choice.*
- *I embrace an intention of "Letting God"—thus receiving the blessings and grace of God's way.*

- *I put my attention upon that which I desire, knowing that manifestation is ongoing in the cycles of life.*
- *I live mindfully so that Truth reveals itself and becomes a way of touching and feeling God.*
- *I see infinite possibilities well beyond a perception of "this or that" and choose the infinite possibilities found in the vibrations of polarity—this and that.*
- *I accept that what I seek in life is somewhere on a continuum of polarity that has flexibility.*
- *I recognize that judgment is unproductive and I choose acceptance and love instead.*
- *I choose to change the frequency of my consciousness vibration to one that is higher.*
- *I see inevitable change in life as part of a natural and Divine process that is predictable and comforting so that I enjoy the cycles of life and rise above suffering.*

Having raised my perception along the polarity of my choice, I give great thanks. Having raised my consciousness, I feel gratitude. I give thanks for all that is of God and love.

I release the energies of these powerful words, knowing that Divine Right Action has been served.

And so it is. Amen.

CHAPTER TEN

Being Whole

The overriding theme, when we use the tools found in the seven principles, takes us in the direction for finding true comfort from within, rather than temporary out-there comfort. After studying each principle separately and coming up with the many tools presented here, I took a look at the whole of it. I had a wonderful revelation when I put the parts together and viewed it more as a journey and state of being rather than merely as an awesome collection of inter-related strategies for living.

It is a case of the whole being greater than the sum of its parts. I observed that the collection of strategies are strategies of their own; leading to a significant way of *being*. It begs to be explored. Helpful in the exploration of being, is a condensed recap of the key aspects of all that we have covered so far in this guide. (It can be used as a quick reference for future use as well.)

Seven Principles Summary

Finding True Inner Comfort is about learning a different direction for easing the discomforts of life. It is about getting to the real inner aspects of "being" instead of being caught up in unhealthy "doing." We have four kinds of reward-seeking:

- Survival Comfort-seeking—mostly normal and necessary.

- Distraction Comfort-seeking—traditional and helpful but has the potential to become mindlessly performed.

- Automatic Comfort-seeking—often harmful in its conscious and mindless versions; a place where addiction lives.

- True Inner Comfort—in contrast to the others, it is a path that looks inward at higher levels of vibration; it is a "being" process instead of a "doing" process.

Affirmation: I consciously seek to lead a life of more being, less doing. I seek comfort from within instead of from out-there.

Principle of Mentalism

"The All is MIND; The Universe is Mental."
—**THE KYBALION**

- God, or The All, is Mind with a capital M. It is unchanging in of itself because it is all. It creates by way of Mind.

- Creation is constant and never-ending. While God does not change, the creative process of God makes for constant change in the Universe. Change is fundamental to life, so resisting change is not productive.

- We know that we are a part of the process of change by way of our own minds; we have the power to change our minds and our feelings by changing our perceptions consciously.

- We can acknowledge and take comfort in knowing that nothing really *is* as everything is *becoming*, so we know "This too shall pass."

Affirmation: All things are becoming and, therefore, changing; I accept change gracefully and adjust my perceptions in order to alter my mind and feelings; I am flexible in my thinking about the evolutionary aspects of life.

Principle of Correspondence

"As above, so below; as below, so above."
—THE KYBALION

- All the good is already in us. Our challenge is to transmute, transform, transcend, and uncover those hidden comforts.

- Whatever is true in the concepts of Earth is true in Heaven and is true in Hell.

- Whatever is true in spirit is true in mind and in physical planes.

- Everything has its own vibration signature.

- There is gratification in taking responsibility in a conscious manner. We are responsible for our lives and what we have created, so we might as well do it from a place of conscious deliberation and with healthy intentions. This allows us choice in generating the next chain of causes and effects in life.

- When we do our best in the Mind's activities, higher energies become reflected in the physical and spiritual planes of life as well.

Affirmation: As I do my best in all efforts, the notion of "As above, so below; as below, so above" is my guide to understanding the commonalities of spiritual, mental, and physical energies in life.

Principle of Vibration

"Nothing rests; everything moves; everything vibrates."
—THE KYBALION

- When we focus our attention upon that which we desire in order to manifest it, that energy pulls similar energy to us. It is wise to focus on what it is that we want, not what we fear.

- When we let go of whatever we are holding on to, we gain freedom from the tension, stress, distress, and the blocks of our thinking and creativity.

- We have the awareness that "Letting God" is allowing the highest vibration to correspond with us on all planes of being, which is a Divine channel to forgiveness.

- Living mindfully brings to us the awareness of Truth and The All on a regular basis.

- We know that practicing mindfulness is about experiencing nowness Reality—a safe place.

Affirmation: Recognizing that all is vibration, I mindfully let go of attachments and embrace the highest spiritual, mental, and physical energies for my daily living.

Principle of Polarity

"Everything is Dual; everything has poles; everything has its pair of opposites; like and unlike are the same; opposites are identical in nature, but different in degrees; extremes meet; all truths are but half-truths; all paradoxes may be reconciled."

—**THE KYBALION**

- There are infinite possibilities and viewing things as either this or that limits our experience and frustrates our life.

- We are aware that "it is what it is." We know that judgment is a human device that creates division, separateness, and uncomfortable feelings.

- Our own willingness and perception have the power to change the direction and level of our consciousness—created by changing our focus within the continuum of our intentions.

- We can ratchet up our vibration by using visualization of a higher vibration of the same class or polarity.

Affirmation: I focus free of judgment on perceived affirmations, knowing that all is on a continuum of varying vibrations and levels of satisfaction.

Principle of Rhythm

"Everything flows, out and in; everything has its tides; all things rise and fall; the pendulum swing manifests in everything; the measure of the swing to the right is the measure of the swing to the left; rhythm compensates."

—THE KYBALION

- Change in life is part of a natural process that is predictable in many ways and therefore not to be feared.

- Cycles of life will continue even as we take charge and rise above them with willful elevation of our own minds from a place of less consciousness to more conscious.

- We can deny the *influence* that the seemingly backward and negative swings of life have over us, thinking to raise our vibration.

- We are aware that pain and suffering are not the result of some "pay up for it" cycle, but instead see that pain and suffering make way for what we see as pleasure and joy.

Affirmation: I know that the cycles and rhythm of life over which I have no control can be purposely overcome mentally by increasing my consciousness about it; I rise above my challenges with my mind.

Principle of Cause and Effect

"Every Cause has its Effect; every Effect has its Cause; everything happens according to Law; Chance is but a name for Law not recognized; there are many planes of causation, but nothing escapes the Law."

—**THE KYBALION**

- Situations in life happen as a result of a long chain of causation with an equal amount of effects.

- Having *expectations* while living in a world of constant change with an immeasurable array of possibilities is a set-up for disappointment. All we can really expect are ongoing changes.

- Chance and luck are terms used in explaining effects we do not perceive.

- We have the power to create our own realities in our minds.

- Blessings and grace from God are the pleasant and unexpected outcomes of cause-and-effect energies being in alignment with the Laws of Nature. It is honoring "Thy will be done."

Affirmation: I am always aware that my mind and mindfulness stimulate cause-and-effect energy, and I use its flexibility to cocreate my life purposefully.

Principle of Gender

> "Gender is in everything; everything has its Masculine and Feminine Principles; Gender manifests on all planes."
> —THE KYBALION

- The nature of God is creatively Masculine and Feminine energy on mental, physical, and spiritual planes.

- Accepting our true nature as vibration-based beings requires us to accept that Feminine and Masculine energies are the essence of all life.

- With both the Masculine and Feminine working in conjunction, mindful action can breed success so that the Feminine and the Masculine fulfill each other.

- The balance between Masculine and Feminine energy creates harmony that then allows for feelings that promote authenticity.

Affirmation: As a spiritual energy force, having mental and physical energy experiences, I embrace and accept myself as a cocreator in life with Masculine and Feminine aspects which are, in fact, the very essence of my authentic character.

FINDING TRUE INNER COMFORT

More Than Just Comfort-seeking Tools

Armed with the knowledge of the seven principles, we are empowered to operate with higher and smarter uses of vibration/energy. Higher vibration equals a more pleasant experience. Using the spiritual and scientific Laws of the Universe is a pretty smart way to live one's life. Instead of fighting, denying, and minimizing these universal laws, we can embrace them, more fully understand them, and allow for finding true inner comfort.

This journey to higher vibration is more than an inward path to peace, joy, and love. Going inward does take us off the expressway most traveled—the road wherein we frantically and frustratingly seek comfort from things outside our True Selves.

Instead, the higher vibration journey takes us down a path much less traveled wherein we find the energies of our Source inside our very being. This really does seem to point to the notion that our lifetime challenge is getting to that godly place. For those with readied ears and willing actions, the higher journey in life is to find and stay on that less-traveled path—the path that does not really lead to God because God is already here within us and ever-present. Ultimately, it is a path to ever-increasing awareness of our Higher Self.

The process of lips to ears related to the seven principles of *The Kybalion* provides a better understanding of the energies that we call God—to our Source by whatever name we choose. A journey to healthy comfort-seeking is a journey to Divine Power's most pleasurable characteristics. This becomes somewhat obvious to the student of the seven principles.

I believe this notion points to the whole that is greater than the sum of its parts. This synergistic point of view is about operating as human beings in such a way that our energies come into alignment with our Source's. It is in this seemingly motionless place that inner joy is found. There is no time or space in that place. It is where God is, what our Source is, what the Force does. It explains why meditation brings peace, enlightenment, and a good sense of being.

The Bigger Question in Life

In seeing the whole of it instead of the sum of all seven principles, one particular "awareness" stands out. It has a comforting aspect to it that is all its own. That aspect is the big question: "What is my purpose in life?" Over the many years of providing addiction and spiritual counseling to individuals, families, and couples, I have repeatedly had this question arise with as many possible answers as there were questioners. And the answers all seemed, at the time, to be rational, relative, and justified for each.

Our Out-There Purpose of Life

Little children often think their purpose in life is about having fun in some sort of play; doing the fun things in life. A lot of adults seem to have hung on to this type of stated purpose. Some make careers out of this—very high-paying careers. For others their purpose is stated as being a good little boy or girl; doing what Mommy and Daddy say. Following the rules and laws falls into that category. And again, many adults cling to this notion. Oftentimes, it is in a more religious way; their purpose is to do the right things and obey the rules set forth by their places of worship. Some folks are more specific with their declared purpose in life. They might state that their purpose is to be the best parent they can be; passing on the honorable and good things of life to their children.

One of the issues I have with these types of purposes is that they tend to be largely based on dualism and out-there aspects of life. There is a basic dualism assumption that there is good and there is bad; a good way of living or a bad one. Dualism thinking is at the root of much of the suffering in life since it is based on the notion that there is man and there is God, as separate from each other. Perceiving ourselves as one gender or another instead of possessing both gender energies is another example. Seeing life aspects as this or that, instead of this *and* that, sets the stage for conflicts on all planes of life. There is a fear of God based on this dualism. Dualism is beautifully detailed in Gary Renard's book *The Disappearance of the Universe.* In it, Renard introduces terms that are archetypal labels that explain the degrees of dualism that exist for mankind. It expounds on the folly of dualism living.

While most well-meaning purposes of life have a certain honorable and positive passion associated with them, they also are charged with possible self-righteous efforts that ultimately become frustrating. This result of dualism is not comforting by any means.

An Inner Purpose in Life

Most purposes in life, as people declare them, are related to what they are *doing* with their lives. It is about "doing" whether in the form of serving, sharing, or gifting or even in less honorable pursuits. From our study of *The Kybalion* and *Finding True Inner Comfort*, we have abandoned that idea of doing for the sake of doing. This is so because "doing" is a frustrating, temporary out-there effort.

Moving from the out-there efforts we can have endeavors that are more Divine in nature. Instead of doing just to do, we would be doing things as a result of *being*. Being the energy of love is perhaps the greatest of the *being* energies. This shift in effort allows us to be less and less concerned with the dual activities of life. Seeing life as more of a dream—or a series of personal stories—we become more focused on *awakening* from the dream stories; being more aware of a greater truth of our nature.

The truth is that we are the maker of the stories that are identified as our lives. By our perceptions, we create. In this awareness, our devotion in life becomes both more and less purposeful. How is this so when we know we don't stop having the roles as a counselor, teacher, preacher, mother, father, and other "doing" roles? The simple answer is we continue those actions with the knowledge that our minds can choose a purpose that is not based on the things of the world, but instead on the only real thing—God, or more specifically God qualities, such as love, peace, and joy. These are the basic qualities of our Inner Self and True Self. The focus on them allows us to remember that we are those inner qualities.

It is thought by many that the Buddha and Jesus, among other great sages, had objectives in life related to nondualism. It is the realization that we and they are pure spirit—pure Mind with a capital M. The manifestations we see and feel in life are relative realities—likely dreams if viewed from the perception of our Source. I would say that a state of non-dualism is another way of saying Christ-like. Buddhists may consider it The Way. There was no question in Jesus's mind that his true nature was of pure spirit. The Buddha, who had a distinctive awareness of this non-dualism would likely have called his purpose to be that of "Awakening." For both, a key intention in life was to *be* aware of their true nature, even while experiencing human form.

One can conclude, then, that to become more Christ-like might be our primary purpose in life. It is to travel the path to awakening and knowing what outer world reality is, as compared to what is Reality with a capital R. It is to see there is no separated self and no individual soul. There is only God; there are only illusions of "not god," and various deceptions of separateness from one another.

Our life's purpose? Maybe to understand that we can experience things in life as if we really are in the world, being busy "doing" in our day-to-day lives; and at the same time, living life awakening to our real Higher Self intention. This stimulates the nature of how we grow and evolve. Being awake means that we know that Spirit or God is all that is True. We have awareness that when we are Awake to the Truth of our being we know all is Spirit.

We can also keep in mind that we can enjoy the process of becoming Awake. What we create in life will naturally be more comforting and pleasing when it is coming from the ongoing place of lessons on how to become Awake and Christ-like.

Sam's Story

The story of a friend of mine shows how a small but significant shift in consciousness can create what he described as "heaven on earth and a life full of miracles." I did not witness his early transformations, since we met later in his life. What I knew, however, was that Sam had been pretty passionate in his spiritual growth. He had wandered from one religious group to another for a decade or so until he happened upon a spiritual group that could not be described as mainstream or traditional.

The teaching of this group resonated with him right from the start. After a few years, he began teaching spiritual truisms, and learned that the more he taught, the deeper he learned the subject matter himself. He was aware that the lessons he ended up teaching were ideas that were embraced by most of the world's mainstream religions; viewing each traditional religion free of its rituals and dogma; thus, stripping each down to the original teachings of the founder.

Sam reached a point wherein he was not interested in the out-there traditions as seen in rituals and dogma. Instead, he had become an avid practitioner of meditation and prayed to the God of his own understanding; one that was not in man's image. This was his way of living when I first met Sam. It was strangely, yet familiarly, much like my own way of living. His way of being resonated with mine.

Sam had become an avid student of "A Course in Miracles." He practiced the lessons every day. From what I could tell, those daily lessons led Sam to an understanding of the importance of forgiveness. Forgiveness became his primary drive in life, until he reached a point where he started describing a new purpose in life. That purpose was to understand and embrace his true nature. He wanted to awaken to the notion that his True Self was that of love, peace, joy, and harmony. He wanted to awaken to the notion that the out-there aspects of life are more like the props, roles, and labels of a play known as My Life—real for experiences, but not Real. He was committed to avoid getting tangled up in just doing life.

The Seven Principles' Ultimate Gift

Sam came to this awareness through his studies in *A Course in Miracles*. As for me, I spent decades getting to the ultimate awareness of my "beingness" largely through my formal and independent studies and, later, through my understanding of *The Kybalion*. As I have always known, there is more than one way get to the Truth. The application of key principles in life helped Sam and me understand that our source is energy—a Source that is really not understandable in full regardless of what we may call It. But we can get closer in our understanding. We can have that journey be our life's purpose. The authors of *The Kybalion* stated this: **"The Principles of Truth are Seven; he who knows these, understandingly, possesses the Magic Key before whose touch all the Doors of the Temple Fly open."**

When we use the principles to such an extent that finding the comfort of God's energies becomes our new norm, we find comfort. Instead of looking to drugs, fancy cars, food, alcohol, sex, status, money, and all the other out-there things for comfort, we *live* the God qualities of love, peace, harmony, and joy. By way of forgiveness, gratitude, and balance, we bridge the out-there with the inner. We step into that energy. There are key distinctions between the lower-vibration things of the world and those things of more pleasurable higher energies; they lead to understanding what Reality is and what Reality is not.

Consider this quote from the Three Initiates: **"The half-wise, recognizing the comparative unreality of the Universe, imagine that they may defy its Laws—such are vain and presumptuous fools, and they are broken against the rocks and torn asunder by the elements by reason of their folly. The truly wise, knowing the nature of the Universe, use Law against Laws; the higher against the lower—escaping the pains of the lower planes by vibrating on the higher. Transmutation, not presumptuous denial, is the weapon of the Master."**

This is saying that we are foolish to think that lower-vibration things of the world go against the Laws of Nature. It is all good. It is saying that the wiser way is to know and use the Laws of Nature. To escape the pain and discomfort of defying those laws, we have the privilege to know them and use them. Some say this is following the statement (taken out of context), "Thy will be done." Thy will be done instead of my will be done.

In wrapping up this study, we can see that using the seven principles, and having a good understanding of them, leads us to a place where we are comfortable enough to consider some rather difficult ideas—namely that our purpose in life can be to accept that life is but a grand stage play in the eyes of God. We are the writer, set designer, director, main character, and star of the stage play known as *My Life*. With all that control, we know that we can ad lib in our own play any time we want.

A more comforting way to be in that stage play is to use our minds with the intention of awakening to the full awareness of the energy we call God, The All, Allah, Mother Nature, the Light, Higher Power, Higher Self, or the Force. It seems wise to change the script sometimes when we find that the story is creating too much drama and not enough joy. *My Life* can be a story of knowing a place of no dualism, to experience Christ-like Oneness and our own full Awakening.

With that mind, I want to conclude by saying that the inspiration from the hundreds of addicted people I have had the honor of serving over the years propelled the writing of *Finding True Inner Comfort*. And I pray that its collective wisdom helps you in finding your own true inner comfort. And I say, Awaken, know Oneness and Be.

Prayer to Self and The All

With humility, I remind myself that God is the Mind.

By way of Mind I know that God and I are One and I create the play known as *My Life*; I have much to say about the nature of that story.

I know that all answers and comforts are found within me.

Without judgment, I accept that change is natural and unavoidable, and also can be mentally overridden.

Without expectations of results, I know I can impact the changes in my life.

With gratitude, I focus my mind on only the energies I desire and those that truly comfort me.

With release of that which is past, I enjoy limitless possibilities that endlessly present themselves.

I accept the love, peace, and joy that are ever-present in me, in all, in God as One.

It is as I believe. It is so. And so it is.

A Guided Meditation

You can take a short trip to Eden or Heaven at any time. The following example of a guided meditation can release you from dualistic thinking and its ramifications. It's a tool for finding true inner comfort.

> Take a few moments and think of something that recently upset or disturbed you. Large or small, see that story. Note your judgment of the facts.
>
> Now visually erase the judgments. Let it just be.
>
> It is what it is. Think to yourself: Is that so?
>
> Smile with the blessing of nonjudgment.
>
> Now consider the ongoing and constantly increasing vibration of something you perceive as "enemy" (such as bullies, victimizers, or terrorists). Consider that the people attracted to this type of behavior are not evil.
>
> Now, let's consider that they are lost people.
>
> They are people looking for love in all the wrong places.
>
> In your mind, you see that love and fear/hate are on the same continuum and, indeed, these misdirected people appear to be living to promote fear and hate.
>
> But let's consider a greater truth; they are seeking power.
>
> See yourself smiling at this misdirected use of energy.
>
> Power and love are not on the same polarity.

Love and power are no more on the same continuum than love and the color purple are.

With the awareness of that Truth, visualize the pole of love.

Fear and hate are terms we use to describe feelings of lack of love. Picture that energy at the end of a pole. See how easy it is for all of us to live in such a place.

Be aware of how fear and hate inadvertently jump to a desire for power over others that we fear.

Consciously visualize moving the energy of the pole of love from that energy which appears as hate and fear—move that energy to higher rates. Will that. See the rate of vibration increase as you stay on the pole of love.

Head for unlimited, unconditional love that knows no bounds—it is toward the highest end of the love pole.

Recognize that your own desires to have power to subdue any bullies' acts of control would be a failed effort because power and love are not on the same pole.

Recognize and feel yourself willing the vibration rate of hate and fear to increase in speed. As the speed increases, we see and feel love.

Feel that love for yourself; that love for your neighbor; that love for all the lost people of Earth—especially those who are lost in the act of using power in order to find the comfort of love.

Imagine all the people feeling love—imagine no ill-perceived need for power over others.

Imagine this judgment-free place. This is your own trip to Eden, Heaven, Nirvana, True Inner Comfort.

Know that you have this ability to be aligned with the energies of God. Accept that everyone, lost and found, has that ability.

See that energy of love growing inside you; growing inside everyone; even those you fear—especially those you fear.

Sense the gratitude for knowing that love triumphs over all.

Allow the energy of love to transform and transmute from what appears to be fear and hate into unconditional love.

Caress the comfort of knowing this higher truth. Know it. Feel it.

Love is all you need. Love is all there is. It is so. And so it is.

Being the Author

Since his teenage years Dr. Don W. Jones was hungry for real solutions to the "stuck" ways of being. From a place of compassion and his own discomforts, he was desperate to find tools to heal unhealthy thoughts and resulting behaviors. In 1989 he discovered the teachings of Ernest Holmes and Thomas Troward and became a fan of their writings on the power of our minds. This led to becoming a student and teacher of New Thought teachings and spiritual education at the Center for Positive Living in Sarasota, Florida. Earning his doctorate in religious studies from Emerson Institute, his cutting-edge study consisted of an intermingled spiritual and quantum mechanics research effort, which explored how our minds and thoughts give power to prayer.

Ordained as an independent New Thought minister, Don acted as spiritual director at the Center for Conscious Living of Northwest Ohio for many years. His talks and workshops inspire people to change their thinking in order to improve their lives as they seek lasting comfort from within.

Complementing these studies, Don's professional education focused on spiritually based cognitive behavioral therapy along with holistic addiction and mental health therapy. As a clinical manager and behavioral health therapist, he has personally assisted hundreds of people in their efforts to find freedom from "dis-eased" beliefs and debilitating addictions. Working with ex-offenders and others with addictions within a faith-based behavioral health treatment center, Don is himself inspired by his clients and their ability to transform their lives by changing their thinking. For more 'Being' information, discussion, and to contact the author visit drdonwjones.com.

www.ingramcontent.com/pod-product-compliance
Lightning Source LLC
Chambersburg PA
CBHW052026070526
44584CB00016B/1915